Santa Barbara

Gayle Baker, Ph.D.

Other works by the author:
  The Wet Mountain Valley, 1975
  Trial and Triumph, 1977
  Catalina Island, 2002

Printed in Canada by Hignell Book Printing

Library of Congress Cataloging in Publication Data:

Baker, Gayle
    Santa Barbara/Gayle Baker, Ph.D.
    1st p. cm. ed.
    Includes index.
    ISBN 0-9710984-1-7
    History of Santa Barbara, California
    I. Title

    PCN 2002114348

Cover by **Larry Iwerks**, *renowned Santa Barbara watercolorist*

All historical photos are from
The Santa Barbara Historical Museum

Table of Contents

The Arrival of the Europeans

Centuries before its recorded history, large numbers of Native Americans lived on the future site of Santa Barbara. These people, known as Chumash, lived in settlements clustered around the pure-water springs in the area. It is estimated that between 8,000 and 10,000 lived and thrived here. They built hive-shaped structures made of tree branches covered by reeds, and ate acorns, seeds, herbs, rabbits, squirrels, fish, and enormous amounts of shellfish. They also enjoyed a treat when a whale washed up on the beach.

They traveled long distances in fast canoes that transported them safely among the Channel Islands and up and down the coast. Most of these canoes held 12 to 15 people and were made of planks carved with care and artistry. These planks were lashed together with fibers and tendons and caulked with the tar found in great quantities along the shore. Although coastal tribes did not have a common language, they traveled so frequently that an intricate and effective system of sign language evolved.

The Spanish Discover the South Coast

Santa Barbara's recorded history began in October 1542, a mere 50 years after Christopher Columbus arrived on the shores of the New World. **Juan Rodriguez Cabrillo** and his crew reached Santa Barbara's south-facing shore in two small, badly-built vessels, the *San Salvador* and the *Victoria.* Cabrillo, a Portuguese sailor employed by the Spanish, saw the future site of Santa Barbara and claimed it for Spain.

Cabrillo was exploring the coast of California in the fruitless search for the Northwest Passage, a large river that would allow ships to sail from the Atlantic to the Pacific. Although this passage was never found, the search for it resulted in the exploration of large portions of the West Coast. On this exploratory journey, Cabrillo also stopped to explore Carpinteria and anchored several miles west of Goleta Point.

As soon as he left to explore the coast north of Santa Barbara, his ships were driven offshore by the treacherous winds in the Santa Barbara Channel. Cabrillo and his crew found refuge in Cuyler's Harbor at San Miguel Island. While he was exploring the island, he fell and injured himself.

From Cuyler's Harbor, Cabrillo and his crew tried several times to sail north. Each time, his ships were blown offshore before rounding Point Conception. Finally, both ships returned to Cuyler's Harbor to wait for the winds to subside.

Unfortunately, Cabrillo's injuries never healed and he died from their complications on San Miguel Island. Many believe he is buried there, but his grave has never been found. Command of the two ships fell to Bartholome Ferrelo.

Finally, the winds calmed and the two ships left Cuyler's Harbor on January 19, 1543. They explored the coast as far north as the Russian River in Oregon before concluding their voyage in Mexico in April 1543. Although this journey set the stage for Santa Barbara's era of Spanish exploration and rule, it was many decades before the Spanish returned to take possession of Santa Barbara.

Sixty years later, **Sebastian Vizcaino** was commissioned to lead another exploratory expedition up the coast of California. As a merchant, rather than a navigator, his appointment was controversial, and many powerful people in Spain felt that he was a poor choice. His fleet of three ships and a crew of 200 left Acapulco in the summer of 1602. Plagued with illness, they voyaged north as quickly as possible.

On December 4, 1602, Vizcaino and his crew anchored off the curving coastline that was to become Santa Barbara. As this was the feast day of Saint Barbara, a legendary Roman martyr and patron saint of sailors, naming the lovely land near the anchorage was an easy choice.

6

Forgotten for a Century

Despite Vizcaino's reports of this scenic land populated with friendly tribes, Spain neglected California until late in the 18th century. By this time, trade had become an important source of a nation's income and it was evident that the country that controlled California's harbors would reap incredible profits. When England, France, and Russia began to covet California's coastline, Spain knew that it was time to assert its ownership.

The first step toward possession of California was to build presidios (forts) at Monterey and San Diego. Once these two presidios had been established, the Spanish began fortifying the coast between San Francisco and San Diego by constructing two more presidios. In addition to strengthening Spain's hold on the province, these presidios provided refuge for the increasing numbers of travelers between San Francisco and San Diego.

In April 1782, soldiers arrived in Santa Barbara with orders to establish the last of these presidios. Their arrival marked the beginning of Santa Barbara's Spanish era.

Spanish Settlement

When **Lieutenant Jose Francisco de Ortega** and his soldiers arrived in Santa Barbara in 1782 to establish the last of the California presidios, they were accompanied by **Padre Junipero Serra**, the kind, dedicated monk credited with the establishment of many California missions. They sought a location that met two specific criteria: a large, friendly native population to work for them, and a consistent source of good water. Although Goleta was the site of the largest native population, it was rejected due to its uncertain water supply. Dos Pueblos had a good supply of water, but had too few Chumash settlements. Santa Barbara had both.

Under orders not to establish a presidio if the tribes were warlike, Ortega was relieved to be welcomed by **Chief Yanonali**, the Chumash chief who led 13 settlements, stretching from Goleta to

7

Carpinteria. Yanonali was born in one of the largest, oldest settlements located on a mound 600 feet inland from the beach between today's Bath and Chapala Streets, later known as Burton's Mound. This area is believed to have been continuously inhabited for over 10,000 years.

According to legend, Yanonali led Ortega to a lush thicket from which bubbled two fine springs of clear water. Although Santa Barbara was plagued by swampy land, these springs at the corner of today's Garden and Ortega Streets (later known as De la Guerra Wells) tipped the scales in favor of building the Presidio at Santa Barbara.

When Yanonali learned that Ortega wanted to build a presidio, he feared that the springs would be overused and leave his people without the water they needed. To reassure him, Ortega brought him gifts. He also brought a promise: he pledged to protect them from attack by the warlike inland valley Tulare tribes.

Eventually, Yanonali's people persuaded him to cooperate with Ortega. Soon they were making adobe bricks for the Presidio and carrying stone for the aqueducts.

The Presidio

Although Ortega selected Santa Barbara because of the spring Yanonali showed him, he did not build the Presidio at the spring. Instead, he avoided the swampy land and mosquitoes by selecting a rise straddling today's intersection of Canon Perdido and Santa Barbara Streets. On April 21, 1782, the birthday of Saint Barbara, Padre Serra formally dedicated the Presidio; praised its perfect location with sweet water, beautiful ocean views, and fertile land; and spoke of the mission that would soon be built. Thirty-six soldiers and several Chumash attended this consecration.

Serra's hopes of building a mission were soon dashed. To his disappointment, the Governor decreed that the mission could not be built until the Presidio had been completed. Old, ill, and discouraged, Serra went back to Monterey to die.

Artist's conception of the Presidio

At first, the Presidio consisted of a crude brush wall surrounding the soldiers' tents. Soon, a chapel, a house for the comandante, barracks for unmarried soldiers, and storage sheds were completed. A roof, made of reeds from the local lagoon, stuck together using the tar from the Carpinteria tar pits, was added.

Progress was slow for a variety of reasons and the Presidio was not completed for many years. Santa Barbara soil was not heavy enough to make strong adobe bricks, so lime had to be dug from the area that is now Hope Ranch, transported to the Presidio, and made into mortar to strengthen the bricks. Additionally, the Chumash were the only source of labor to build the Presidio and to cultivate the surrounding land. Not used to the grueling and regimented work, many Chumash balked and ran away or sickened.

Despite these challenges, slow but steady progress was made. By 1793, the Governor of California announced that Santa Barbara's Presidio was the best in California. When it was finally completed in 1797, the Presidio wall enclosed approximately a city block. Cannon were placed at each corner of the main gate and the reed roof had been replaced with red clay tiles.

Although it was charged with both military and civil jurisdiction over a large area from Lompoc to Los Angeles, Santa Barbara's Presidio was never a well-provisioned outpost. By 1811, Spanish ships, always rare, stopped coming entirely. Hungry and ragged soldiers waited hopelessly for supplies and wages. By 1813, the Comandante officially informed the Governor that his soldiers had been shirtless, underfed, and unpaid for the past three years. Amazingly, despite this neglect, the soldiers remained loyal to Spain.

The Mission

By 1785, two years after Serra's death and many years before the Presidio was completed, the Governor relented and plans were made to build Santa Barbara's Mission. When **Padre Fermin la Lasuen** and two friars arrived in 1786 to begin building, they rejected the Montecito site that had been selected and chose the higher ground near Mission Creek.

The dedication was planned for December 4, 1786, the feast day of Saint Barbara. When the day arrived, the Governor had not yet arrived, but Padre Lasuen proceeded with the dedication by raising a wooden cross, saying a Mass, and lighting the altar candles so that the Mission could claim Saint Barbara's day as its official establishment date. These altar candles have remained lit since this dedication, making it California's only continuously functioning mission. When the Governor arrived 10 days later, another celebration was held.

Initially, Santa Barbara's Mission was a crude hut. The chapel, constructed of poles and thatch, was completed almost immediately. Soon, the bells sent from Mexico by the King of Spain were strung between poles to call worshipers to services.

During the first six months, 70 Chumash were baptized. Those who came to live at the Mission were called "neophytes" and were taught religion, woodworking, farming, cooking, building, and weaving. Within a year, 307 neophytes lived at the Mission and had built an adobe chapel, a friars' home, a granary, a kitchen, a carpentry shop, and a tannery. Animals and seed contributed by other missions thrived so that during this first year, fields were cultivated and herds flourished to number 80 cows, 27 sheep, 87 goats, 32 horses, and 9 mules.

Unlike the Presidio, characterized by hungry, ragged, and unpaid soldiers, Santa Barbara's Mission was immediately successful, achieving almost complete self-sufficiency. The Mission continued to flourish for the remainder of the 18th century, and by the close of the century, a reservoir, 3 granaries, a leather shop, a blacksmith shop, and storehouses had been built. Approximately 800 Chumash families lived and worked there. For years, Yanonali had refused to be converted to Christianity. Finally in 1787 he relented, and was baptized "Pedro." He died at the Mission at age 68 in 1805.

The completion of the Mission was delayed by a series of earthquakes. Beginning in December 1812 and continuing until March 1813, these earthquakes caused much structural damage and required extensive

Mission, circa 1887

rebuilding. The Mission was finally completed in 1820, 34 years after it had been established. Its dedication on September 10, 1820 was celebrated with fireworks, musicians, and dancers.

Mission Land

The Mission had the luxury of one resource that was virtually unlimited—land. With the exception of small plots given as a reward to high-ranking soldiers, the Mission controlled all the land in the region. These vast holdings were divided into a number of "ranchos."

In theory, the Church was holding this land in trust for the neophytes. The plan was that as soon as the neophytes had learned to cultivate it, ownership of all the land would revert to them. Until this time, these enormous tracts of land, rich with crops and herds, were used to support the Mission. Although the King of Spain continued to hope that the Chumash would be rapidly converted and freed to cultivate their land, many knew that the flourishing Mission structure was too powerful a force to disappear soon.

During the Mission's first 40 years, its wealth, influence, size, and power far outweighed that of the Presidio. As their goals were often at odds, Santa Barbara's early years were marked by steadily growing feelings of resentment between its military and religious institutions.

Illness Plagues the Mission's Neophytes

Despite its wealth, by the beginning of the 19th century, a cycle of disease began that would eventually cripple the Mission. In 1801, a serious outbreak of pneumonia in Santa Barbara killed both soldiers and neophytes. Although many soldiers died during this epidemic, the toll was far higher for the neophytes.

Neophytes who survived this pneumonia outbreak soon found themselves ill from a wide variety of other diseases carried by the Spanish. By 1812, it was clear that far too many neophytes were dying of such common illnesses as colds and measles. Also, birthrates had dropped significantly and many babies did not survive childhood. The padres were forced to face the fact that the Chumash were not thriving in their new role as Christians.

By the time the Mission was completed in 1820, its decline had already begun. Since the Mission was dependent on large numbers of healthy neophytes for its prosperity, their illnesses and declining birth rates foretold its demise. The Mission's power deteriorated quickly while tensions between the religious Mission community and the secular Presidio community grew. When Mexico gained possession of California, the takeover of the Mission and its enormous tracts of land was just around the corner.

Santa Barbara's Founding Families

Some of the original 36 soldiers and 9 scouts of the Presidio brought their wives and families from Mexico with them. Few of them returned to Mexico when their army days were over. Most stayed in Santa Barbara, creating Santa Barbara's founding families.

These families were permitted to build homes outside the Presidio walls. They created a hodgepodge of adobes clustered around the Presidio. Eventually these families, plus the families of a few sailors and traders, had established a tiny community. By 1793, when Vancouver passed through on one of his exploratory journeys, he reported a firmly established community with adequate food.

During these early years, Santa Barbara was an unpleasant place to live. The adobes surrounding the Presidio were dirty, ugly, and odorous. None had glass in their windows, and when the wind blew, dust permeated everything. Garbage and waste lay rotting for rats and seagulls, which performed the only refuse removal services for the young town. Not surprisingly, on hot days, Santa Barbara stunk.

Santa Barbara's Presidio Comandantes, especially **Captain Jose Francisco de Ortega** and **Don Jose De la Guerra y Noriega,** played significant roles in transforming this rough and dirty village into a cleaner, more pleasant town.

13

Ortega was a skilled engineer who was also fun-loving, overweight, and unwise with money. He established the Presidio in 1782 and served as its Comandante until he was ordered back to Mexico in 1784. Under his command, irrigation ditches were dug so land could be cultivated. Before long, these irrigation ditches nurtured the vegetable gardens, vineyards, and orchards dotting the young Santa Barbara's landscape.

Eventually, Ortega's two weaknesses, obesity and poor money management, left him penniless and jobless. He was forced to seek early retirement at 61, after 36 years of service, because he was so overweight that he could no longer mount his horse. Unfortunately, he was also deeply in debt to the Spanish government.

He asked for some land so that he could raise cattle and eventually pay off his debt. Although the Mission held the land in trust for the Chumash, the Governor agreed to allow him to select some land to work so that he could repay the government. He was warned that this land would revert to the government as soon as he died. He selected land near Refugio.

Ignoring the missionaries' adamant opposition to this private use of land, Ortega moved his wife and 8 children there and built an adobe home, barns, and a corral. Almost immediately, he planted vineyards, fruits, and vegetables and began acquiring cattle. As his sons matured, they each built adobes in adjoining canyons up the coast. Eventually, the Ortegas had settled land stretching 25 miles along the coast near Refugio.

Soon after Ortega moved to Refugio, his money problems were over. He had stumbled into an extremely lucrative trade opportunity. As luck would have it, Refugio was a favorite anchorage for Yankee ships smuggling goods into California. Although this trade was illegal, Ortega was eager to trade and sold his fruits, vegetables, and cowhides to the smugglers.

In exchange for these local goods, Ortega acquired silks and spices from China, shoes and cloth from Peru, and tables and chairs from

New England. He then sold these illegal treasures to soldiers, who had been forgotten and unpaid by Spain for many years and felt no compulsion to enforce Spanish laws. Before long, all soldiers who could afford them had jewelry, clothes, mahogany furniture, and expensive Chinese rugs from Ortega's treasure trove.

When Ortega died in 1798 at 65, his sons stayed. Thirty-six years later, when the missions were secularized, the Ortegas were granted 26,529 acres of coastal land.

Don Jose De la Guerra y Noriega

While the important and wealthy Ortegas were characterized by energy, fun, and a most liberal interpretation of the law, another of Santa Barbara's important founding families, the De la Guerras, was known for their grace and charm. Don Jose De la Guerra y Noriega came to California in 1806 and became a lieutenant at the Presidio. He fell in love with and married Dona Maria Antonia Juliana Carrillo. Dona Maria soon became known as a gracious and affectionate wife, mother, and hostess. According to legend, one

De la Guerra Adobe, circa 1867

American visitor said there were two things in California that were supremely good: Dona Maria and grapes.

When De la Guerra became the Comandante of the Presidio, he and his family built a home next to it. This home became the center of the town's political and social life. During Santa Barbara's Spanish era, it was the site of numerous resplendent celebrations and gatherings. Respectable and courtly, the De la Guerras epitomized pastoral charm and set the standard of behavior for early Santa Barbara society.

De la Guerra is credited with transforming an arid area into the first of the many verdant gardens that distinguish Santa Barbara today. He planted eight acres of gardens and orchards near the spring that Yanonali had shown to Ortega. This spring soon became known as De la Guerra Wells, and today's Garden Street was so named because it bisected these wonderful gardens.

These families established the foundation of the town that Santa Barbara was to become. Together, the soldiers with their adobes clustered around the Presidio and the wealthy founding families such as the Ortegas and De la Guerras, gave Santa Barbara a distinctive Spanish character that remains evident today.

Pirates, Trappers, and Smugglers

According to legend, De la Guerra's courtly manners are credited with helping to foil a pirate's plans to loot California's coastal towns. While he was imprisoned in Santa Barbara in 1816, Captain Henry Gyzellar was so impressed with De la Guerra's courtesy that he returned two years later to warn De la Guerra of an imminent attack by a pirate, **Captain Hipolito de Bouchard**.

Bouchard was an admiral serving Argentina, then a colony fighting for its independence from Spain. Gyzellar had observed him outfitting two frigates in Hawaii and bragging about his plans to attack California ports. Under the guise of striking a blow against Argentina's enemy, Spain, Bouchard hoped these attacks would net him holds filled with precious booty.

16

As soon as De la Guerra heard of the impending attack, he sent a messenger to Monterey to warn the provincial capital. When Bouchard and 280 heavily armed men arrived in Monterey, on November 22, 1818, demanding the surrender of the provincial capital, most citizens had fled. Bouchard burned and looted homes. After sacking the capital, he headed south with the intention of looting the rich Rancho Refugio and Santa Barbara. Citizens prepared for attack by sending wives and children to the Santa Ines Mission and hiding valuables in the surrounding mountains. As Bouchard approached, they watched and waited.

Bouchard and his ships were sighted off Gaviota on December 2, 1818. **Sergeant Carrillo** and 30 soldiers rushed to Refugio as Bouchard's frigates, with large cannon pointing toward land, anchored near the rancho. Several small boats with armed pirates rowed ashore while Carrillo and his men hid in the brush and waited.

When Bouchard and his men came ashore, they found the rancho deserted. When three of the pirates strayed from the house into the vineyard, Carrillo's men lassoed them and dragged them into the brush. When other pirates tried to rescue them, Carrillo's men began firing from their hiding places.

Bouchard and his small band returned to their ships, but came back the next day with more men. By this time, neophytes from the Mission had arrived to help repel Bouchard's attack. They hid with Carrillo's men and watched. Bouchard and his men burned and looted the rancho, slaughtered all the cattle they could catch, and returned to their ship vowing to destroy Santa Barbara next.

As Bouchard's frigates headed east, Carrillo and his men followed on foot along the coast, watching and waiting for the next attack. Two days later, Bouchard and his men anchored just off Santa Barbara and prepared to attack.

The odds were in favor of Bouchard: 280 pirates to 50 soldiers; 40 large cannon to the Presidio's two small cannon. Carrillo knew his only hope was to fool Bouchard into thinking he had many more soldiers and weapons than he actually had.

He had a plan to do just that: Carrillo gathered his 50 soldiers on the beach and organized them into a march. Each soldier rode from behind the willows into full view of Bouchard, disappeared behind a nearby knoll and circled back to do it again. While hidden behind the knoll, they changed shirts and hats in addition to changing their order of formation so that neither they nor their horses would be recognized.

Carrillo was counting on Bouchard to be watching and hoped he would count the same men over and over and over again. It worked! Bouchard sent an officer ashore under a white truce flag saying: "We can easily batter your adobe houses into dust with our cannon balls. But all we are after is our three men. Give back your prisoners and we will sail away." De la Guerra, the Presidio Comandante, agreed. The prisoners were released, and Bouchard sailed south. He was sighted near San Juan Capistrano briefly and was never seen again.

One footnote to Santa Barbara's pirate tale: one of the three captured pirates was an American, **Joseph Chapman**. He returned to become one of Santa Barbara's most famous foreign residents. He epitomized the typical Yankee: smart, competent, and popular. Eventually, he wooed and married Guadalupe Ortega, whose ranch Bouchard had looted and burned. Descendants of Joseph and Guadalupe still reside in Santa Barbara, and Joseph is buried at the Mission.

Trappers and Smugglers

During Santa Barbara's Spanish years, the young village flourished in an era characterized by a gracious, pastoral society, the strong presence of the Church, and enough isolation from Spain to develop a character uniquely its own.

One advantage of Santa Barbara's isolation from Spain was the ability of residents to ignore laws they did not like. The lucrative and thriving trapping and smuggling operations offer prime examples of Spain's inability to enforce its laws.

Trapping was illegal for all but Spanish nationals. Despite this prohibition, large numbers of non-Spanish trappers from Russia,

England and America s Rocky Mountains came to Santa Barbara regularly. Their quarry, the sea otter, was numerous and easy to catch and their pelts brought a whopping $30 in Honolulu and $90 in China. In the face of these enormous profits, trappers found it easy to ignore Spain s anti-trapping law. Soon, Santa Barbara was one of the most profitable trapping locations in the world.

Russians were among the first to enter California waters seeking fur seal and sea otter pelts. As early as 1741, a Russian ship took 900 sea otter skins back to make the cloaks so prized by Russia s aristocracy and royalty.

Before long, word of the rich waters reached American trappers in the Rocky Mouintains. These Rocky Mountain trappers were boistrous, hard living, hard fighting and independent. Most left Santa Barbara as soon as their trapping was done, but some stayed. These Americans introduced a new, energetic, and unpolished element to the young settlement that was markedly different from that of the Spanish soldiers.

Soon this wholesale massacre of sea otter resulted in their disappearance from seas around Santa Barbara. Trappers, forced to find another source of income, looked to the other illegal and lucrative activity smuggling. Conditions were perfect for smuggling to flourish for several reasons:

> The law imposing an enormous tax on all non-Spanish ships was not enforced.

> The cattle hides sought by smugglers abounded. Previously valueless, these hides, with the advent of smugglers, routinely brought an impressive $2 each.

> Smuggled products were needed in Santa Barbara. These Eastern seaboard goods were essential as there was virtually no local production. With no local coal, no year-round streams large enough to provide power, and none of the metals so valued by industry in the East, manufacturing was difficult, if not impossible.

New England ships would bring coveted products from the East, hide them in coves on Santa Cruz Island, and gradually smuggle them to Santa Barbara. Hides and tallow would then be surreptitiously loaded, and these untaxed ships would be on their way home with chests full of money and holds full of hides and tallow.

Trading hides and tallow was the perfect solution to Santa Barbara's inability to manufacture its own products and before long, smuggling became its economic foundation. Officials closed their eyes to this smuggling, while respected soldiers, clergy, and leading citizens bought, sold, and profited.

For many, these were good years: Santa Barbara basked in welcome isolation from Spanish rule with hides to sell, valued Eastern goods to buy, and a constant flow of interesting ships from all over the world. They liked this pastoral life and were unsupportive of Mexico's agitation for freedom. It was only when Mexico declared its independence from Spain in 1821 that citizens were forced to face the fact that it was about to become a Mexican territory.

Mexico Ushers in Cowboy Era

After years of agitation, Mexico won its independence from Spain in 1821. When a messenger brought the astounding news that Spain no longer ruled Santa Barbara, many watched in horror as numerous new laws were imposed. A constitution adopted in 1824 required banishment for all who refused to take an oath of loyalty to Mexico. By 1827, a law had been passed requiring deportation of all who had been born in Spain, were less than 60 years of age, and did not have a Mexican wife.

Although it appeared that these laws would bring significant changes to Santa Barbara's largely Spanish population, many were relieved that these laws were seldom enforced. In most cases, they were evoked only when a Mexican politician needed them to get rid of an opponent.

Mexico was so disorganized that it was able to neither control nor support California. The large number of Mexican governors who failed in their attempts to rule California illustrates this disarray. In the 25 years of Mexican rule, there were 13 different governors. In many cases, the Santa Barbara streets named for them, such as Sola, Victoria, and Figueroa, were their most memorable contributions to California history.

The years of Mexican rule were characterized by the development of large, privately owned ranchos, replete with cowboys. Almost immediately, a society dominated by the Mission and the Presidio was replaced by a social structure dominated by these powerful ranchos.

The Fate of the Chumash

Soon after Mexico gained possession of California, the neighboring war-like Tulares encouraged the Chumash throughout the South

Coast to revolt. Plans for this revolt were made, and bows and arrows were crafted and hidden. The spark that ignited the revolution was the cruel flogging of a neophyte by a soldier at the Santa Ines Mission in February 1824. The Santa Ines neophytes revolted. Although soldiers sent a cry for help to Santa Barbara, by the time soldiers arrived, most of Santa Ines Mission had been burned.

The revolt spread to La Purisima Mission, near today's Lompoc, where tribes, fearful they would be attacked, drove soldiers into the church. After a battle that raged all night, seven Chumash, four soldiers, and one Spanish woman had been shot. Soldiers surrendered in exchange for their safety and left the Chumash in control of La Purisima. Several weeks later, they gave their weapons to the padres and began working in the fields again.

In Santa Barbara, neophytes hid in the Mission tower with bows and arrows. The soldiers quickly took control of the Mission, killing three neophytes. According to legend, soldiers then went back to the Presidio for lunch, taunting them with, "We will be back as soon as we have had our chocolate . . . We will bring a cannon and blow you all sky high."

Fearful, the neophytes decided to take their families and journey inland to join the Tulare tribe. Soldiers, angry when they returned to find that they had left the Mission, destroyed their adobe homes and their crops, food supplies, and animals. They even killed four old Chumash who were travelling from Dos Pueblos and knew nothing of the revolt.

In March, De la Guerra sent 80 soldiers inland to find the runaway neophytes and bring them back. They found them near the city of Maricopa and killed four of them. The rest escaped, and the soldiers returned to Santa Barbara to face an angry and disappointed De la Guerra. By summer, a gentle priest journeyed inland to visit his neophytes. He found them disheartened and ill and talked them into giving up their bows and arrows and returning to the Mission.

Neophytes returned to even worse conditions than they had left. Although many criticize the treatment they received by the

Spanish, most agree that their lot was even worse under Mexican rule. This era is marked by forced labor, whippings, poor food, and inadequate medical treatment. During the years of Mexican rule, a large percentage of the surviving Chumash in Santa Barbara died from malnutrition and disease. Combined with a plummeting birth rate and high infant mortality, the Mexican era marked the low point of the once proud and flourishing Chumash of the Santa Barbara region.

Secularization of the Missions

Under Spanish rule, most of the land was owned and controlled by the church through its missions. To many soldiers and settlers, it appeared that the padres had all the land, resources, and power. They chafed under the apparent unfairness of this inequity.

Mexican rule brought an end to the mission system. In 1833, the Mexican Congress adopted a *Decree of Secularization* that mandated all missions be converted to parish churches and the vast mission resources, except the church itself, be transferred to the government. Throughout California, padres were removed and replaced by curates.

The huge tracts of land comprising the mission ranchos were dispersed. In Santa Barbara, much of this land was offered to Chumash neophytes who successfully occupied and cultivated it for two years. In addition to the land, these neophytes were given one-half of the Mission's grain, cattle, and equipment. Although designed to give them independence, the plan was a complete failure. Some sold their land or were cheated out of it, and most eventually left to work on other ranchos or joined the inland Tulare tribe. Virtually none who remained successfully gained self-sufficiency through the cultivation of this land.

During this transition, much that had been developed under the mission system was destroyed. Before long, the wealthy resources of Santa Barbara Mission lay in ruins: huge herds were running wild and left to starve; cultivated lands reverted to the wild; and much of the equipment was stolen or left to rot.

Huge tracts of Mission land were parceled up and given or sold to soldiers and settlers. Suddenly, Santa Barbara was transformed from a church-dominated culture into a society dominated by affluent rancheros (ranch owners) and the cowboys who worked these ranchos.

Santa Barbara Mission suffered less that other missions. In 1840, the first bishop appointed as the leader of the new Mexican parish church system, **Francisco Garcia Diego**, selected Santa Barbara Mission as his residence. His arrival in 1842 brought much excitement and celebration. As his residence, the Mission was protected from the destruction that plagued many of California's other missions.

Nevertheless, by 1845, when it was clear that Mexico would lose California to the United States, **Pio Pico**, the last Mexican governor, began selling missions to the highest bidders. Again, Santa Barbara Mission was lucky: Americans Daniel Hill and his son-in-law, Richard Den, staunch supporters of the church, bought the Mission and surrounding land from Pio Pico for $7,500, with hopes of saving it. They allowed the clergy to stay and continue services. By the 1860s, the California Supreme Court had declared this sale illegal and deeded the Santa Barbara Mission, including the church, its garden, and the cemetery, back to the Catholic Church.

The Birth of the Ranchos

The 25 years of political turmoil and uncertainty under Mexican rule changed the face of Santa Barbara forever. Each of the 13 Mexican governors needed allies to quell hostilities and build coalitions. They soon found that giving large tracts of land was an effective way to buy loyalty. Though these land grants were not technically legal until they were approved by the Mexican government, locally these grants were considered binding.

Much of the area that is now Santa Barbara County was divided into 40 large ranchos. Even Santa Cruz and Santa Rosa Islands were given as land grants. The only area not parceled into ranchos was the coastal land between Goleta and the Rincon, except for Hope Ranch.

These coastal lands were, instead, designated "pueblo lands" belonging to the young towns. Before long, the only land not allocated were the mountain areas too steep for sheep to graze and the windswept Santa Maria Valley.

Ranchos soon became the dominant social, political, and economic force of the region. Presidio officers were given their first choice of these large tracts of land. Next, powerful Santa Barbara citizens were given tracts. Although one had to be a Mexican citizen to acquire land, this was not a deterrent: wealthy Santa Barbara residents simply found a way to acquire Mexican citizenship. Soon citizens were owners of huge tracts of land, and Santa Barbara had become the home of a group of wealthy ranchers, called rancheros.

By Mexican law, a rancho could not be larger than 49,000 acres. Many assumed that these tracts would remain large and that a few wealthy men would continue to own most of the land. This assumption was incorrect. Unlike the English Law of Primogeniture that required all land to pass intact to the oldest son, when the rancho owner died, land was divided between his wife and each of their numerous children. Within a few generations, most of these huge ranchos had been divided into relatively small tracts of land.

Although many do not see Santa Barbara's "Mexican Years" as golden ones, others recalled this ranching era with fondness. Characterized by Mexican cowboys, celebrations, and resplendent clothes, it is remembered as a time of fiestas, exuberant high spirits, rodeos, and wealth for those lucky few landowners.

Santa Barbara's golden ranching days did not last long. By the summer of 1846, the United States had declared war on Mexico. This marked the beginning of the end of Santa Barbara's rancho days and the transition from an isolated village to a vibrant American town.

The Yankees

Smuggling continued to flourish during these Mexican years. In hopes of getting rich from California's growing trade, the Mexican government passed a law prohibiting all but Mexican-owned vessels to trade. While this law was even more severe than the Spanish law requiring exorbitant duties on non-Spanish vessels, it was seldom enforced. Before long, ships from the Eastern seaboard were arriving regularly in Santa Barbara. When these ships, richly stocked with desperately needed manufactured goods, anchored off Santa Barbara's shoreline, even law-abiding citizens flocked to buy. After selling their goods, ship captains were thrilled to refill their holds with Santa Barbara produce and hides.

This lucrative trade brought Americans to Santa Barbara. Although most came to trade and left, many fell in love with Santa Barbara and stayed. Almost overnight, these Yankees became an extremely powerful force in Santa Barbara.

Many of these Yankees stayed because they fell in love with Spanish girls. They wooed and married the daughters of Santa Barbara's leading Spanish citizens. The five daughters of Carrillo became the brides of Americans, while three of the four De la Guerra daughters also married Yankees. Did these wealthy fathers realize that the future of Santa Barbara rested with enterprising, energetic Americans and methodically pair their daughters with these future leaders?

Steeped in tradition and ceremony, many of these weddings were lavish affairs. The wedding of one of De la Guerra's daughters, Ana Maria, to the American, Alfred Robinson, was documented and made famous by Richard Henry Dana's description of it in *Two Years Before the Mast*.

In order to marry, Americans had to convert to Catholicism and gain Mexican citizenship. Mexican citizenship also entitled them to acquire land. As a result, many of these Americans-turned-Mexican soon acquired rich ranchos. Before long, "Yankee Dons," with their lovely, cultured, and wealthy Spanish wives, had become Santa Barbara's leading citizens.

Not all the Americans who came to Santa Barbara and stayed became model citizens. Other waves of immigrants left an entirely different mark on the Santa Barbara region. In addition to the fur trappers who came by foot from the Rocky Mountains, whalers found wealth in the waters of the Santa Barbara Channel.

Before the discovery of kerosene, whale oil lit lamps throughout the world. When observers realized that Santa Barbara was a perfect location to catch migrating whales, the whaling ships arrived. Many of these whalers came from long distances, often as far as Maine or Rhode Island. They remained in the Santa Barbara Channel for two to three years, until their holds were full of oil, before returning home.

The whalers waited in ships near Point Conception watching for the distinctive blow of whales. As soon as whales were sighted, a crew in a small boat rowed the harpooner toward the whale. If the harpooner was skilled, the whale was harpooned and dove deep to die. A few days later, the dead whale surfaced, and the whalers cut the thick layer of yellow fat (blubber) into chunks.

The chunks were melted into oil in 70-gallon iron kettles on the beach. These kettles were stored at whaling stations such as the large one in Goleta where Ward Memorial Boulevard is today. When oil was discovered in Pennsylvania in 1859, kerosene began to replace whale oil, and whaling declined. The last whaling station in Santa Barbara was closed by 1890.

Like the traders, trappers and whalers were energetic and ambitious. Instead of marrying the daughters of the wealthy and adopting the local culture, they remained quintessentially American. They brought an energy, independence, and directness that shocked the polished and aristocratic Spanish families. They expected the United States to claim the lush, promise-filled land called California and were waiting for Santa Barbara to become an American town.

The End of the Mexican Era

The years of Mexican rule were characterized by such continuous political turmoil in Mexico that Santa Barbara was virtually forgotten. Resentful and restless citizens repeatedly asked the Yankees who had settled in Santa Barbara why it was taking the United States so long to take possession of California.

Forgotten by Mexico, Santa Barbara was also repeatedly buffeted by disparate California interests. During these years, California was comprised of a long strip of largely independent settlements stretching from San Diego to San Francisco. Each of these settlements had different needs and perspectives. Each village wanted to become California's most important town and was willing to fight for this prize.

Between the strong anti-Mexican sentiments of San Francisco and Monterey and pro-Mexican settlements in Los Angeles and San Diego, Santa Barbara was often caught in the middle. An example of this is the attempt of an ex-convict, **Joaquin Solis**, to gain California's independence from Mexico. In 1829, Solis convinced the soldiers in Monterey, who had not been paid for years, to march south to fight for independence from Mexico. The Governor of California sent troops north from San Diego to meet Solis's soldiers. As both forces approached Santa Barbara, local support wavered between Mexican and anti-Mexican sentiments. By the time these two armies arrived, as many as 30 women had rowed through the surf to seek refuge in a ship anchored offshore while most other Santa Barbara citizens were hiding in the Presidio.

A battle took place three to four miles west of Santa Barbara. After three days of fighting, the only casualty was one horse, and Solis had run out of ammunition and supplies. He retreated north, watching helplessly as his troops deserted and dispersed. He was finally captured in Monterey. Although it was known as the "Battle of Santa Barbara," most view this battle as a comedy of errors and incompetence.

Although Mexico weathered this challenge, it was soon clear that the Mexican dominance would not last long. Local leaders knew that close alignment to the Americans in Santa Barbara was smart.

The Americans Arrive

As war between Mexico and the United States loomed, Santa Barbara's loyalties were divided. Still primarily dominated by powerful Spanish families with little respect for Mexican politicians, many were cautiously supportive of an American takeover. Naturally, Americans enthusiastically supported a United States victory over Mexico. Despite these anti-Mexican sentiments, Santa Barbara was also the home of a significant number of Mexicans who were committed to fight a takeover by the United States. As a result, Santa Barbara's response to the war between Mexico and America was full of contradictions. American troops were welcomed, wined, dined, chased, and attacked.

The Mexican-American War began in July 1846, when an American warship, *Congress*, captured Monterey, causing the Mexican governor, Pio Pico, to flee for Mexico. Journeying south to capture all of California, *Congress* had arrived in Santa Barbara by August. On August 4, 1846, *Congress*'s captain, **Commodore Robert Stockton**, and 10 United States Marines rowed ashore and marched to the Presidio to accept Santa Barbara's surrender. Americans in Santa Barbara were gleeful, while many Mexicans were so afraid that they fled to the Mission for protection. Most citizens simply watched with curiosity, anxious to discover if Yankee rule would be good for Santa Barbara.

The last Mexican comandante of the Presidio, **Colonel Gumesindo Flores**, surrendered to Stockton and his troops and escorted them as they replaced the Mexican flag with the American ensign. When they arrived, the Mexican flag had disappeared. Nearly three-quarters of a century later, on her 100th birthday, Flores' wife, Dona Cipriana Llanos de Flores, admitted that she had hidden the Mexican flag so that it would not be disgraced. She later gave the fine wool flag to a poor mother to clothe her children.

As soon as he had officially relieved Flores of his post, Stockton left Midshipman William Mitchell and 9 of his Marines in command of Santa Barbara and sailed south to capture Los Angeles. Santa Barbara citizens liked them, especially Mitchell, and soon settled down to their normal peaceful life. When Stockton returned in September, he found Santa Barbara so tranquil that he took Mitchell and his men with him as he continued on his journey of conquest.

Unrest in Santa Barbara

When it appeared that surrender of California was complete and American troops had been dispersed throughout California, unrest flared to the south. Pro-Mexican soldiers in Los Angeles attacked American troops and chased them to San Pedro. This ignited a spark of dissatisfaction with the American takeover that spread throughout California. In Santa Barbara, Mexican citizens burned the United States flag and threatened to kill all Yankees.

When **Lieutenant John C. Fremont** and his troops stopped at Santa Barbara, Yankee residents told him they were fearful. To quell their concerns, Fremont agreed to leave **Lieutenant Theodore Talbot** and nine soldiers in Santa Barbara to protect them.

For awhile, Talbot and his men lived peacefully in Santa Barbara. He and his troops were well liked by local citizens. Unfortunately, word spread to Los Angeles, the hotbed of the rebellion, that an undermanned troop of United States soldiers had been left in Santa Barbara. Before long, 200 Mexicans came from Los Angeles to kill Talbot and his men.

When pro-American citizens in Santa Barbara learned of the approaching troops, they warned Talbot and his men to hide in Mission Canyon and gave them food and blankets. The Mexicans followed them into the canyon. When they could not catch them, they torched the bushes to smoke them out, but Talbot and his troops escaped and hiked to Monterey.

By the fall of 1846, Mexican troops had retaken Los Angeles, and Fremont journeyed south to fight the Mexican loyalists. He had 450 foot soldiers, many of whom had no uniforms but wore buckskins or jeans. Since he had to pass Santa Barbara, he decided to take the opportunity to punish citizens for chasing his troops out of town. Not knowing that some citizens had helped the American troops to escape, he vowed to level every house in Santa Barbara.

Fremont began his march south on November 30. Rains were early that year, and the route consisted of over 300 miles of mud-filled gulches and raging streams. Troops were forced to build rafts to cross streams that had been dry gulches just weeks earlier, and could only travel 15 miles a day. Feed for the pack animals was so scarce that many died, and soon soldiers were dragging their artillery through the mud.

Exhausted, Fremont and his men camped for three weeks a few miles north of Gaviota Pass near the rancho of **Benjamin Foxen**, an English sailor, trader, and shipbuilder turned rancher. They rested and ate the rancho's plentiful fresh beef before continuing their journey south.

During these weeks of rest and replenishment, legend has it that Foxen told Fremont that rebels were waiting for him at Gaviota Pass, a narrow pass flanked by sheer walls of granite. Fremont was told that as soon as he and his men were in the canyon, the rebels were going to blast boulders with gunpowder, killing as many as possible and imprisoning the rest. According to this legend, Foxen and his son offered to guide Fremont and his troops over the treacherous San Marcos Pass.

Rebels were not hiding in wait but had gone south to join General Pico's army in Los Angeles, and it is unclear whether Foxen even told Fremont that the rebels were waiting there. It is clear, however, that, for some reason, Fremont selected the rough route over San Marcos Pass rather than entering Santa Barbara via the far simpler route over Gaviota Pass.

It was a terrible journey. Christmas morning brought a huge storm. Horses and men slipped and struggled, inching their way over the steep muddy pass. By the time they had reached the outskirts of Santa Barbara, their cannon had plummeted down a ravine, 150 horses and mules had died, and most of their provisions had been jettisoned into the canyon.

After a short rest, on December 27, Fremont and his men marched into Santa Barbara. No shot was fired, and the invasion was peaceful and courteous.

Many Santa Barbara citizens were delighted to see their friend Lieutenant Talbot among the tired troop of Americans. They had feared that he and his men had died and were joyful to learn that all had escaped. Talbot was given the honor of hoisting the United States flag.

Santa Barbara citizens treated Foxen as a traitor. His rancho was burned three times, and his cattle and horses were repeatedly stampeded. He finally left his beloved rancho and did not return until seven years later when tempers had cooled enough for him to resume his life. An unanswered question: Did Foxen give Fremont information he knew was incorrect to convince American troops to select the most dangerous and difficult route into Santa Barbara? Whatever his motivation, the result of Foxen's "help" brought hardship and devastating losses to the American troops.

After resting for a week, behaving civilly to citizens, and relenting on his vow to burn Santa Barbara to the ground, Fremont and his soldiers marched on Los Angeles to fight Pio Pico and his Mexican troops. Instead, Pico met them at Cahuenga Pass with a white flag of surrender. The Mexican War officially ended January 13, 1847, although fighting continued in California for another year. California now belonged to the United States, and Santa Barbara was about to change dramatically.

By April 1847, 300 Americans had been stationed in Santa Barbara. They were there to keep order and, more importantly, to take an active role in the development of the new American town. They were members of an unusual regiment of New York volunteers under the command of **J. D. Stevenson**. During 1846, volunteers had been recruited to serve in the Mexican-American War, with the understanding that they would stay and settle when the war had been won.

By the time Stevenson's volunteers arrived, the war had ended. They stayed to fulfill their second charge, the colonization of Santa Barbara. Many of these volunteers played important roles in the young town although they were not all model citizens; one became Santa Barbara's most infamous bandit, Jack Powers. These rambunctious young men brought energy, playfulness, and none of the culture and courtliness so prized in Santa Barbara.

According to legend, they also brought baseball. Residents of this lazy Spanish town were horrified when wild balls escaped the baseball diamond at State and Cota Streets and outfielders casually trampled gardens and knocked laundry lines into the mud chasing them. The Americanization of Santa Barbara had begun.

First Steps Toward Americanization

Santa Barbara was incorporated as a city on April 9, 1850, five months before California became a state. Despite this speedy incorporation, Santa Barbara had a long way to go to become a smoothly functioning city. Not only was there no funding for city government, but no newspaper publicized government actions and there were no public meeting sites. Nevertheless, a Common Council, charged with running the loosely connected jumble of adobes called Santa Barbara, was soon elected and began meeting in makeshift rooms.

Generating the funds to pay the salary of a clerk to manage the day-to-day operations of the town was a top priority. Council moved rapidly to generate these funds by requiring licenses of every business. Of the first 50 businesses licensed, 32 were a markedly American institution: saloons. These fees quickly generated the income necessary to hire a clerk and establish the new city's treasury.

Although the city coffers were filling, the Council remained rigidly thrifty. Records show that $50 was allocated for all operating expenses, including initial purchases to set up an office with bookshelves and stationery. Extravagances were strictly forbidden.

Another source of income rapidly increased Santa Barbara's treasury. Under Spanish rule, the church had owned all land. Under Mexican rule, land was given to reward the loyalty of some and to buy that of others. As soon as the United States took control, Santa Barbara land was for sale to all who could afford it. As residents scrambled to buy, money flowed into the city treasury. During Santa Barbara's first 15 years, Council parceled out so much land that most agreed that Council's only accomplishment was the selling of Santa Barbara.

And such bargains were to be had! Swampy beach land sold for 75 cents per acre. In 1856, three city lots were sold for $1; others sold for from $5 to $50. In 1863, Thomas Hope purchased a 200-acre tract on the Mesa for $100. Land in Montecito often sold for 75 cents an acre, but records indicate that 96 acres in Montecito sold for 50 cents an acre in 1863. Carpinteria land prices averaged 25 cents per acre.

Without a newspaper, the Clerk of the Council made two copies of all Council actions and posted one on the corner of a home at Cabrillo and Chapala and the other in front of the local billiard parlor.

The Santa Barbara of 1850 was languishing in a gentle serenity in its little backwater valley. Concerns centered on local, pastoral interests. Council reflected this slow-moving culture. Much action was postponed, and the Council quickly gained a reputation for procrastination. Even getting the Councilmen to attend meetings was somewhat of a challenge. For example, between May and August 1853, the clerk recorded 15 meetings with no one in attendance.

During these early years, Santa Barbara, although American, retained the flavor of a Spanish town. Despite the rambunctious energy brought by many of the Yankees, charm, pride, and manners were still highly valued. The dignity and gracious form that had characterized the Spanish rule continued throughout Santa Barbara's initial years as an American town. Spanish remained the language of choice in most Santa Barbara homes and, although by 1852 Council minutes were kept in English, Spanish was the official language of records until 1870.

While Yankees have been blamed for destroying the romantic, charming, pastoral Santa Barbara, they also brought a commitment to education that was not present in Old California. Under Spanish and Mexican rule, education was not valued as much as style and good horsemanship for boys, and charm, fine embroidery, and sweet singing for girls. Only a small percentage of the population, mainly the rich and the clergy, knew how to read and write. On the other hand, in 1850 only one out of six Americans was illiterate.

The first American school began in 1849, before Santa Barbara was incorporated. The teacher was promised $70 per month to teach 20 boys. As there was no money, the clerk gave up his salary so that these boys could learn. When Santa Barbara became an American city in 1850, the Council began paying for this teacher. The school only survived until 1852, but another was established by 1854. By June 1855, 70 boys had enrolled in the new school.

Despite the success of these private schools, the development of a public school system in Santa Barbara faced some serious challenges. In 1854, California established a state school system, and most towns received funding to establish a school. Unfortunately, Santa Barbara did not receive these funds. It seems that a required report was never submitted. Citizens worked energetically to recover this appropriation, but many other California towns did not support Santa Barbara's appeal.

These towns fought to keep Santa Barbara from getting state money for education because of the deplorable state of its schools. They noted that Santa Barbara did not even have a schoolhouse, but used a damp, poorly lighted room in the Presidio for classes. They also noted that students had no books and that classes were not conducted in English.

After this shaky beginning, progress toward developing a state-approved school system in Santa Barbara was understandably slow. Throughout much of the 1800s, numerous small private schools opened, struggled, and closed.

Survey and Street Plan

Santa Barbara's first neighborhood was comprised of adobes scattered haphazardly around the Presidio. By 1850, the number of adobes had increased, but they were still built on sites with no apparent organization. Americans brought with them a passion for organization and knew that a logical street system was an essential first step. In 1851, the Common Council authorized **Captain Salisbury Haley** to survey and plat streets in square, uniform blocks 150 feet wide.

Although the streets laid out by Haley are the ones we use today, it took many decades for Santa Barbara's streets to conform to his survey. This survey resulted in streets that looked great on paper, but, unfortunately, many of Haley's streets were drawn through existing buildings. Rather than tear down all buildings that had the bad luck of being in the middle of one of Haley's streets, the Council allowed Santa Barbara's streets to zig and zag around these dwellings. It took years before the buildings in the middle of Haley's surveyed streets were torn or fell down and the streets were straightened to conform to the survey. Eventually, the streets Haley drew did emerge, but, until recently, even State Street jogged around the Raffoer Hotel.

Unfortunately, Haley was a more skilled seaman than engineer. Two decades later it was discovered that the blocks he platted varied in size. Blocks near the starting point were fine, but they got progressively smaller until blocks at the edges of town were only 120 feet wide. He had lacked the proper surveying instruments and had used measuring chains made of leather. Santa Barbara's foggy mornings and hot afternoons stretched and shrank the leather so its length on cold wet mornings was significantly different from its length on hot afternoons. The result was Santa Barbara blocks of widely differing sizes.

36

Despite this error, once the city was surveyed, civic pride grew. Although streets were still treacherous and muddy, Santa Barbara citizens began to envision a town rather than a jumble of adobe homes. By 1855, three public squares, plus Plaza de la Guerra, Plaza Vera Cruz, and the Alameda, had been completed.

Santa Barbara's Wonderful Street Names

The Council appointed three leading citizens to name her newly platted streets; **Antonio Maria De la Guerra**, **Joaquin Carrillo**, and **Eugene Lies**. They did an extraordinarily good job of preserving Santa Barbara's charm by selecting names that captured history and tradition. They honored city founders and prominent citizens (Ortega, De la Guerra, Carrillo, Gutierrez, Cota), respected Chumash chiefs (Anapamu and Yanonali), four Mexican governors (Figueroa, Victoria, Sola, Micheltorena), and one American governor (Richard B. Mason).

Although there are dozens of wonderful names, one of Santa Barbara's most interesting street names is Canon Perdido, so called for the lost cannon. In the winter 1847, just after the United States had taken possession of California, the American brig, *Elizabeth*, was wrecked on the beach at Santa Barbara. Its cannon was left on the beach, and by May it had disappeared. Afraid that pro-Mexican citizens had taken it to attack the American troops, the captain in charge sent a cry for help to the government in Monterey. In response, Governor Mason demanded that Santa Barbara citizens be fined $500 for the missing gun.

Believing this to be a ridiculous fine, citizens offered the money during the Fourth of July festivities and transformed the punishment into an opportunity to laugh and celebrate. A decade later, in 1858, the cannon was found burned on the beach. Citizens hauled it out and ceremoniously paraded it through the town.

Both the street named Canon Perdido and the cannon on Santa Barbara's first official seal marks this event, an illustration of Santa Barbara citizens' dignity and humor, in contrast to the serious demeanor of the Yankees. This cannon appears on the seal with the inscription: "Vale 500 P." Translated as "Worth $500" or, when translated as Latin, "Goodbye $500," the humor of this incident lives on.

Americans and Their Homes

One sign of the transformation of Santa Barbara was the evolving preference for lumber over adobe. Yankees had a preconceived notion of what a home should look like and the carpentry skills to build their homes. They went to great lengths to get their logs. Many arrived on the decks of schooners, while others were floated down the coast. All were propelled through the surf onto the beach.

Most locals watched in wonder and horror as Yankees rejected adobe and selected wood as their building material of choice. They knew adobe was inexpensive, durable, and both wonderfully cool in the summer and warm in winter. They also hated to see shingles replace their wonderful tiles. Not only were these tiles the perfect roofing material for Santa Barbara, but they were also a romantic favorite. According to a legend of highly questionable authenticity, these tiles had been originally shaped over the thighs of shapely Chumash maidens.

Alpheus Thompson built one of Santa Barbara's first frame houses in 1851. He had lumber for the house brought by schooner from South America and floated ashore. Legend has it that the house burned down the day it was completed when the housewarming ball to celebrate its completion turned into a house burning. It was told that an angry local resident, trying to stop the wooden house fad, had set fire to it.

Soon, **Captain John Smith**, married to one of the Ortega daughters, built a frame house that survived a bit longer. Located on De la Guerra Street, it lasted until the mid-1920s when the Board of Education ordered it razed to make room for a school building.

The first American mansion was built by **Judge Albert Packard**. Packard settled in Santa Barbara in the 1850s on a choice 200-acre parcel fronting on De la Vina Street, bounded by Canon Perdido and Micheltorena Streets, extending toward the Mesa. Before long, the mansion he built there replaced Casa De la Guerra as the social center of the young town.

An avid horticulturist, he landscaped his estate with rare and wonderful plants, such as Sicilian lemons and limes, avocados, cherimoyas (custard apples), apples, pears, and loquats. He devoted most of his property to grapes. Eventually, he was producing 80,000 gallons of wine each year and marketing it in Europe.

When the "Anaheim Disease" destroyed his grapes, he planted olives. He also imported silkworms, planted groves of mulberry bushes to feed his silkworms, and began producing cocoons in the attic of his winery. The silkworms thrived, but, unfortunately, the cocoons still needed to be sent to Japan for processing. The cost of this processing rendered his budding silk company economically untenable. Although Packard's silk production experiment was short-lived, it did result in providing silk for California's first state flag.

After three decades of agricultural enterprise, Packard left Santa Barbara in disgust when, in 1887, the Southern Pacific put rails through the center of his lovely palm-lined driveway. Eventually, Packard did return to Santa Barbara to live out the last years of his life, and is buried in the Santa Barbara Cemetery.

Communication Victories and Challenges

On May 24, 1855, Santa Barbara got its first newspaper, the *Santa Barbara Gazette*. Half in Spanish and half in English, it offered citizens welcome information ranging from legal notices and news to local happenings and bargain specials. It symbolized a new era for the town that had depended on informal information sources for so many years.

During these years, regularly scheduled steamers journeying up and down the coast of California visited Santa Barbara. Without a wharf, Santa Barbara was a challenging place to land. Many who tried were soaked by the rough surf or even dumped into the frigid water as their rowboats were being beached. Despite these difficulties, this transportation link and the visitors it brought marked an important step toward combating Santa Barbara's isolation.

In addition to bringing Santa Barbara's first tourists, these steamers also carried mail. Unfortunately, to the intense frustration of citizens, the mail contractor routinely failed to deliver Santa Barbara's mail. Citizens watched helplessly as their precious mail traveled up and down the coast repeatedly until the contractor was willing to risk rowing it through the surf.

Even when the mail was rowed ashore, the mail sacks were often left on the beach. Unless helpful passersby carried them to town, many of these mail sacks were swept out to sea and lost forever. During these years, Santa Barbara citizens agonized over innumerable letters, newspapers, and legal documents that never reached the Santa Barbara Post Office.

Santa Barbara citizens were annoyed by their isolation. They embraced their future as a vibrant American town and wanted all the benefits that being American could offer, including regular mail service, a wharf, and, most of all, a railroad. Although some of these amenities came relatively quickly, Santa Barbara faced an excruciatingly long wait for its most important link, a railroad.

Gold Rush Years

Although gold was never discovered in Santa Barbara's hills, California's 1849 Gold Rush had a significant impact on the young town. It ushered in both a financial boom and an era of lawlessness. While many were working to transform Santa Barbara into a thoroughly American town by developing city government, streets, schools, newspapers, and homes, the Gold Rush interferred with that progress.

Before California's Gold Rush, the major cash value of cattle had been in the hides and tallow that had been traded to smugglers for Eastern goods. When California's population ballooned during the Gold Rush, cattle became an essential food source. Gold-seeking prospectors needed beef and were willing to pay dearly for it. Almost overnight, trade in cattle was transformed from that of hides and tallow to that of beef for food. Huge herds were driven to San Francisco, and wealth poured into the pockets of Santa Barbara

Mule riders on State Street

rancheros. For 15 years, they dominated the financial, political, and social life of Santa Barbara. Although Santa Barbara had just become an American town, the Gold Rush ushered in an era marked by prosperity (for the rancheros), genteel parties, and an air of slow-moving sophistication patterned on old Spanish ways.

Outlaws

More than cattle drives, rodeos, and fiestas marked Santa Barbara's cowboy era. It also brought an entirely new challenge: lawlessness. Although most arrived at the gold fields by sea through San Francisco, many came from the south. Suddenly, Santa Barbara found itself on the route of prospectors rushing north to the gold fields.

These gold-seekers spent money in Santa Barbara on their way to and from the gold fields. They loved the grace and prosperity of Santa Barbara, and many stayed to play in the numerous, lively saloons. Santa Barbara coffers were enriched, but many felt invaded by this vibrant parade of prospectors.

Soon, these gambling and drinking establishments became the center of a host of illegal activities. City officials were unprepared to control this lawlessness, and by the early 1850s, criminal activity had grown into a serious problem.

Several well-known outlaws led this criminal activity. Santa Barbara's first genuine bandito was **Salomon Pico**, cousin of the powerful Mexican-era family. Initially, those with loyalty to Mexico saw his attacks on Americans as both romantic and appealing. In the minds of these Mexican loyalists, Americans were still the enemy. As a result, Pico's robberies were initially accepted and even encouraged by many. Protected by his good family name, he was never punished in Santa Barbara, but later was executed in Baja California.

Santa Barbara also hosted one of California's most spectacular bandits, **Jack Powers**. Powers had arrived in California as a member of Stevenson's New York Volunteers, the group recruited to settle in Santa Barbara as soon as America had won the war with Mexico. While a New York Volunteer, he began his career as a master gambler. Powers was a brilliant gambler, with the manners of a gentleman, the looks of a Hollywood movie star, award-winning horsemanship skills, charm, and charisma. Before long, Powers had become a political force with influence over a succession of California governors. In the eyes of many, he was a hero.

With intentions of settling in Santa Barbara, Powers squatted on abandoned property owned by Richard Den, the man who had purchased the Mission from Mexico to save it from ruin. When the sheriff came to eject him, Powers and his gang gathered behind the ruined walls of the ranch house and fought off the sheriff. Men on both sides were killed before the sheriff retreated, and Powers retained his illegal possession of Den's land.

Powers' outlaw band terrorized travelers on the El Camino Real. Their targets were rich prospectors returning from the gold fields. They were headquartered close to the old "Outlaw Tree" near today's North Ontare Road and State Street. Legends tell of undiscovered caches of stolen gold still buried in this area.

By 1855, Powers had reached the zenith of his power and the sheriff and mayor had resigned in frustration. A lone county judge wrote warrants to establish some semblance of order, but no officers remained in Santa Barbara to make the arrests.

The negligent tolerance of these outlaws, plus the inability to enforce order, established the roots of widespread lawlessness that engulfed Santa Barbara. In 1855, it was more dangerous to travel from Santa Barbara to San Luis Obispo than anywhere else along the entire California coast.

Each week brought tales of more violence. Crimes escalated from robbery to murder, and mangled bodies were routinely left along the trail. Travelers were warned never to travel after dark, never to trust local strangers, and to ride quickly away from Santa Barbara.

Finally, vigilantes from San Luis Obispo had had enough. Fifty determined riders dressed in red flannel shirts and white straw hats came to Santa Barbara to find Powers. He fled, never to return, and died an ignominious death in Sonora a few years later. His gang drifted apart after losing its fearful leader.

Although the disbanding of Powers' gang brought some peace to the surrounding countryside, Santa Barbara was not yet a law-abiding community. It's significant that it took vigilantes from another town to defeat Jack Powers. Local law and order was virtually non-existent. Santa Barbara's government simply could not govern, courts did not function, and elected officials were helpless.

By 1860, the chaos was so prevalent that city government had virtually disappeared. Santa Barbara's reputation as a dangerous place persisted until 1861, when the California State Legislature established a new city government. This reorganization was successful and brought the first peace since the Gold Rush had rocked Santa Barbara 12 years earlier. Under the influence of this new government, peace, opportunity, and a sense of local pride thrived. Santa Barbara was becoming an established, functioning city.

Tales of Buried Treasure

Although Santa Barbara's lawless years had ended, exciting stories of buried treasure have been passed on through the generations. One favorite is the tale of pirates landing at Hendry's Beach and traveling inland up the Arroyo Burro to bury a chest of gold and jewels under a tree. Some say an old treasure map identifies this tree on the east bank of San Roque Creek and State Street, near today's Burger King. Treasure seekers continue to dig all around it. If anyone has found any treasure, no one is telling. Many suspect that this treasure remains buried under one of the huge nearby stumps.

In another of Santa Barbara's treasure tales, **James H. Wall** came to California in 1851 from Australia, carrying $20,000 worth of jewels in his money belt. After drinking too much one evening, he told **Joaquin Murieta**, a local Montecito bandit, about his wealth. Murietta killed Wall. He buried the jewels somewhere in the Santa Barbara area and drew a map identifying their location.

James's son, **David Wall**, got his hands on this treasure map after Murieta's death in 1853, but never searched for the jewels. In 1886 David came to Santa Barbara to work as a gardener. One day, he showed the map to his employer. Together, they began tracking down landmarks for fun. Finally, they found the spot near Rincon Creek. They began digging and soon found a rusty iron box filled with diamonds, sapphires, and emeralds. Valued at between $13,000 and $14,000, some of these jewels were identified as among those David's father had brought from Australia almost 40 years earlier.

Although Santa Barbara did not have its own gold rush, the young city experienced the wealth, lawlessness, and tales of treasure that characterized so many of America's boomtowns during the Gold Rush years.

Civil War Years

Santa Barbara Tries to Join the War

From 1860 to 1865, the United States was being torn apart. The Union Army fought to preserve the United States, while the Confederate Army fought with equal fervor to establish an independent Southern slave-holding nation. While thousands of Americans died, Santa Barbara citizens, over 3,000 miles from the fighting, chafed under their isolation.

As the Civil War raged, citizens waited, watched, and wondered. News of battles came with each stagecoach and steamer. Unfortunately, this news was at least 20 to 30 days old by the time it arrived. Although the news was old, it was all Santa Barbara could get. When a stagecoach was due to arrive, throngs waited anxiously on State Street, hungering for news of the devastating battles raging on the opposite coast of the nation.

Santa Barbara's loyalties were divided. Although there were strong Confederate sympathies, most of those with political power wanted Santa Barbara to become a Union town. They believed that the only way to accomplish this was to get the Union Army to send troops to Santa Barbara. When this request was delivered to Washington, the Union Army immediately refused, stating that the protection of Santa Barbara citizens loyal to the Union was not a priority. The message was clear: whether Santa Barbara supported the North or the South was of little interest to the Union Army. Santa Barbara was on its own and unimportant to the war effort.

Despite this rebuff, an ardent Union supporter, **Don Antonio Maria De la Guerra**, a former Santa Barbara mayor, a California senator, and a respected city leader, formed a company of 84 Union volunteers. This company was comprised of 83 citizens of Spanish decent and one Anglo. The support of the De la Guerra family was unmistakable, for, in addition to the leadership of Don Antonio Maria, three other De la Guerras also served.

By August 1864, this troop marched out of Santa Barbara to help save the Union. They were the only Union troop that did not speak the language of the nation for which they had committed to fight. They began marching south, and 10 days later, on September 2, 1864, they reached General Winfield Scott's camp in Wilmington. There they were declared a cavalry company and waited to be called to action.

After months of waiting in Wilmington, they began a trek to Arizona. By this time, the war was drawing to a close, and the Union Army no longer needed these distant troops. After waiting several more months along the route east, they were called to San Francisco to be mustered out and sent home to Santa Barbara. Their only taste of war had been a bloodless skirmish in Arizona against a band of raiding Apaches.

Their failure to reach the battle was a bitter disappointment, for it signified Santa Barbara's isolation and unimportance. Nevertheless, citizens reacted to the return of their soldiers in the way they knew best—they celebrated! Citizens waited joyfully on the beach as the troops arrived. Cheering crowds and bands greeted them and escorted them up State Street.

In retrospect, although Santa Barbara citizens were sorely disappointed that their troops had not played a glorious role in the war, government officials were impressed that these brave men were willing to dash across the nation to help. In later years, this support was fondly remembered in Washington. And, though still isolated and relatively unimportant, Santa Barbara gained the reputation of a community of gutsy, brave, and loyal citizens.

Drought and Devastation

In 1863, the first in a series of severe droughts swept the region. Cattle by the thousands herded around disappearing water holes and slowly died of thirst and starvation. The land had become so dry that grass simply could not grow. After three successive seasons of drought, leaving the land strewn with dead cattle, it was clear that the days of the large, prosperous ranchos had ended.

Where 200,000 cattle had thrived in 1863, by the time the rains came back three years later, only 5,000 survived. The financial loss was devastating. In addition to the enormous losses resulting from the death of cattle, land values plummeted. Huge ranchos were, suddenly, practically worthless. The value of rangeland fell so low that, in some cases, it was worth only 10 cents an acre.

This period of drought marked the end of the dominance of Santa Barbara's cattle barons. They watched stoically as they saw their life of respectability, influence, and wealth disappear forever. Drought also brought an abrupt halt to Santa Barbara's prime industry, cattle, and marked the end of the era of affluent, pastoral life remembered as "Old California."

While many lamented the end of Santa Barbara's ranching era, it forced the break-up of the great ranchos. These original land grants were partitioned into small parcels and sold for practically nothing. This cheap land enticed new groups of businessmen, entrepreneurs and small farmers to Santa Barbara. By 1869, most of the ranchos were gone, and land nearest Santa Barbara was slowly being converted to small farms and some light industry.

With this abundance of cheap land and the arrival of entrepreneurs, many predicted that Santa Barbara was about to enter a new era of growth and prosperity. All that was needed was the arrival of the transcontinental railroad to realize this promise.

Santa Barbara's citizens watched as the railroad slowly inched its way across the nation.

Looking west from Chapala Pier

Political activity on State Street

Nineteenth Century America

While Santa Barbara citizens waited anxiously for the railroad as it creeped across the West, the entrepreneurs did not wait. They arrived by ship and fell in love with the placid little California town with its genteel and leisurely old Spanish traditions.

They were not as charmed by Santa Barbara's amenities. They lamented its lack of a wharf, a dependable water supply, paved roads, and orderly streets. They complained that entry had to be made by rowing small boats through the surf, water came from wells, and roads were often muddy. They immediately set to work transforming this sleepy little town that they had found so appealing.

These new residents brought energy, enterprise, talent, intellect, culture, good business instincts, and a civic vision. Many of them also brought enough wealth to turn these visions into reality. Under the leadership of men like **Colonel William Hollister**, **Ellwood Cooper**, and **John P. Stearns**, Santa Barbara was transformed almost overnight.

Rutted, muddy State Street

Mule team grading State Street

New buildings sprang up, and welcome improvements were made. In 1869, Santa Barbara College, Southern California's first co-ed prep school, was opened in the San Marcos Building at State and Anapamu Streets and, by 1872, State Street was graded and street lamps were installed.

Tired of waiting for news from stagecoaches or ships, citizens purchased $2,245 worth of stock in a company that would build a telegraph line. On September 28, 1870, Santa Barbara citizens received their first message. They rejoiced in being connected to the rest of the world and celebrated this first step toward vanquishing their isolation.

These entrepreneurs believed fervently that Santa Barbara would soon become one of the great commercial cities of the West. During countless meetings, flamboyant speakers prophesized Santa Barbara's brilliant future and wealth.

Transportation Woes

The only thing blocking this promise was its lack of a railroad; for, as everyone knew, to become a great commercial city, one needed a railroad. Until it arrived, all knew that Santa Barbara was destined to remain isolated and forgotten.

On May 10, 1869, the transcontinental railroad was completed with a symbolic golden spike and jubilant celebrations. Unfortunately, its terminus in San Francisco was still woefully distant from Santa Barbara. Nevertheless, citizens were determined to lure a spur to their town. Unfortunately, they were able to offer little to entice the railroad magnates to make the enormous investment necessary to extend the railroad over the rough terrain between Santa Barbara and San Francisco. Santa Barbara simply did not produce any unique products that would make this railway connection profitable.

First train from the south, 1887

It was not until 1887 that it was completed from the south to Ellwood and another 14 years until, on March 31, 1901, Santa Barbara was finally connected to San Francisco by rail. Without a rail connection for so many decades, Santa Barbara leaders were forced to give up their dream of becoming one of California's leading commercial centers. Instead, they began to bank on Santa Barbara's isolation and beauty to draw tourists and their dollars.

During the long years of waiting for the railroad to reach Santa Barbara, citizens had to depend on ships and stagecoaches for their connection to the world. Although stagecoaches and steamers served Santa Barbara regularly, the settler's vehicle of choice, the Conestoga wagon, or prairie schooner, was never able to make it to Santa Barbara. These wagons were too bulky to go over the mountains that blockaded the town and could not go around them at Gaviota to the north, or Rincon to the south.

If they had been able to come, it is likely that Santa Barbara emigration patterns would have looked much like those of a number of other rapidly growing California towns. As it was, those who came to Santa Barbara did not come by the thousands in heavy wagons with all their possessions prepared to establish farms. Instead, smaller numbers of more affluent visitors arrived, traveling lightly by ship or stagecoach. Most came only to visit. Many stayed.

Over the years, travelers had arrived in Santa Barbara by sea on a wide variety of boats, including canoes, junks, schooners, square-rigged clipper ships, and warships. As schooners began to disappear, side-wheel steamboats began puffing and wallowing up and down the coast from San Francisco to Los Angeles.

SS *Orizaba*

The *Orizaba*, one of these side-wheeled steamers, brought many of Santa Barbara's early visitors. It was known for its erratic schedule and its propensity for arriving in the middle of the night. People awaiting its passengers spent many hours on the beach at night shivering, annoyed, and wondering when the overdue *Orizaba* would finally arrive.

West Beach from Castillo Point

Although an important seacoast town, Santa Barbara had no harbor. Its lovely curved coastline was scenic, but offered ships little protection. All ship captains who anchored along the coast just beyond the kelp knew they had to be ready to pull their anchor at a moment's notice. Many passengers had a shock when they came to the beach to board and found that their ship had left.

Even when the weather cooperated, landing was difficult. Until 1865, passengers and cargoes had to be rowed ashore through the breakers and kelp. Many passengers got an unexpected shower or dip in the ocean. Precious cargoes were routinely lost overboard. . . . Something clearly had to be done.

Stearns Wharf, circa 1875

In 1865, a group of city leaders joined to form the first Santa Barbara Wharf Company and received permission from City Council to build the town's much-needed wharf. They built a primitive wharf at the foot of Chapala Street. Although it was a step in the right direction, it was simply not long enough to reach deep water. No vessel over 100 tons dared tie up to it.

It was soon clear that Santa Barbara needed a better wharf, and **John P. Stearns** began to make plans to build one. By 1872, Stearns Wharf was complete, and on September 16, 1872, the first steamship tied up to it, and citizens celebrated. Stearns Wharf still serves Santa Barbara visitors and locals alike with its shops and fine restaurants.

Despite the great convenience offered by the wharf, Santa Barbara remained a fair-weather harbor with an acute need for a breakwater. In 1873, Santa Barbara citizens sought Federal funds to build a deep-water harbor and a breakwater. Congress would not allocate funds for this project, and the need for a breakwater remained unmet.

During December 1878, storms destroyed and washed away more than 1,000 feet of Stearns Wharf. Nevertheless, it would be 52 years before Santa Barbara would get its breakwater.

A Landmark takes Root

Santa Barbara's entrepreneurs brought amenities and comforts. Alongside the improvements, however, were disturbing signs that Santa Barbara was beginning to look like any other American town.

Although Santa Barbara was looking more and more American, remnants of her Spanish roots remained. Rather than blending, Santa Barbara spent the last few decades of the 19th century with a confused hodgepodge of ornate Victorian buildings and Spanish adobes.

During these years of rapid change, a Santa Barbara landmark was taking root and flourishing. In 1876, as the story goes, a little girl who lived at 201 State Street got a seedling of a Moreton Bay fig tree from an Australian sailor. She planted it on July 4th, America's 100th birthday. When she moved the following year, she asked her friend, Adeline Crabb, to transplant it to her home at the corner of Chapala and Montecito Streets.

This seedling, a cousin of the rubber tree and not really a fig at all, grew and grew and grew. Still thriving, it is believed to be the largest of its species in the world, with a root system that spans over an acre. Surviving Standard Oil's plans to chop it down to build a service station and impressing Nikita Khrushchev when he visited Santa Barbara in 1959, generations of citizens and tourists alike have marveled at this wondrous tree.

Tourist and Health Mecca

Santa Barbara's isolation, the source of such frustration to its citizens, played a major role in determining its future. Its mountain barrier had stopped the tidal waves of immigrants that flooded so many California towns after the Civil War. While other California towns were becoming large and prosperous commercial centers, Santa Barbara remained small and forgotten.

By the late 1860s, this isolation, though still inconvenient and annoying, began to transform Santa Barbara into a remote and romantic destination for the rich and adventurous. Isolation, plus

Original Los Banos on present site of Pershing Park

Santa Barbara's beautiful surroundings, great climate, and small town Spanish flavor, began to attract an extraordinarily interesting group of visitors.

Initially, many of these visitors were seeking a cure for their ills. A common theory was that salt air mixed with petroleum fumes cured illness. It was widely accepted that the Channel winds that blew over the large oil slick hugging the coast gave Santa Barbara the purest of air and the perfect location for therapy. An added bonus was the healing, hot sulfur springs that abounded in Santa Barbara. These bountiful springs, plus the healthful air, attracted health seekers from all over the world.

Not all who came were ill. One visitor was **Charles Nordhoff**, a writer subsidized by Southern Pacific Railroad to travel around California and publish his impressions. He visited Santa Barbara during the winter of 1872 and was he ever impressed!

As soon as he returned to the East, he wrote *California—a Book for Travelers and Settlers*. He glowingly described Santa Barbara and its potential as a health resort, tourist destination, and agricultural center. The book was an instant best seller. He wrote,

> *"Santa Barbara is on many accounts the pleasantest of all the places I have named . . . . Santa Barbara has the advantages of pleasant society and an excellent school. It is, in fact, a cozy nest of New England and Western New York people, many of whom originally came here for their health, and remain because they are charmed by the climate!"*

His description of Santa Barbara as the world's most ideal health and tourist resort transformed this quiet town. The following winter, Santa Barbara was flooded by an unbelievable number of unexpected visitors. Rich travelers, seeking genteel society in a mild winter climate, journeyers seeking adventure off the beaten path, and invalids in desperate health poured into Santa Barbara. Hotels could not accommodate the 80 to 100 visitors who arrived each day. Some believe that an entirely new sort of traveler, the tourist, was born in Santa Barbara during that winter of 1873.

Santa Barbara's hotels were few and spartan. It was clear to Santa Barbara's entrepreneurs that visitors needed somewhere to play and stay and that there was money to be made satisfying this need. Led by **Colonel Charles Hollister**, one of Santa Barbara's prominent citizens, investors were eager to supply the funds to build Santa Barbara's first elegant hotel. Speed was of the essence, and efforts to raise money that began in July 1874 resulted in the opening of the Arlington Hotel, on State Street between Victoria and Sola, by July 1875. The cost for this 90-room luxury hotel was $170,000; furnishings added another $30,000.

The Arlington Hotel appeared to be an instant hit, for it was filled and profitable its first season. Unfortunately, the high costs expended to build it so quickly took their toll. Although the Arlington was the hub of Santa Barbara's elite tourist society, its financial success was short-lived. Before long, investors pulled out, and Colonel Hollister became its sole owner.

Original Arlington Hotel built in 1875

Hollister took an active role promoting his new hotel. As legend tells it, when the *Orizaba* arrived and representatives of Santa Barbara's hotels clustered around the passengers to woo them to their hotels, Hollister stood back quietly watching. He silently separated the rich arrivals from the others. With a tiny gesture of his hand, he identified the rich passengers to his drivers who proceeded to herd them to the Arlington Hotel.

As the wealthy came to Santa Barbara, an entirely new group of workers was needed to serve them. Luring these workers to Santa Barbara was not hard, but finding housing for them soon became a problem. To begin to address this need, an old-fashioned boarding house was built in 1871 outside town at 1404 De la Vina. It boasted 10 bedrooms, 3 bathrooms with hot and cold water, a large stable, and a surrey that provided taxi service to town each hour.

Before long, it had gained a reputation for excellent cuisine, and tourists who could not afford the Arlington began to stay there alongside the workers. Originally called Lincoln House, it was purchased by **Cyrus Upham** after a succession of owners. Today known as the Upham Hotel, it is Santa Barbara's oldest, continuously operating hotel.

"All the Amenities of an Eastern Town . . ."

And the tourists kept coming. Rich visitors told their friends about the delights of Santa Barbara, and every year more arrived. Almost immediately, this quiet old Spanish town changed its entire focus. Santa Barbara citizens became completely absorbed in attending to the wants and desires of wealthy tourists.

Santa Barbara leaders made the assumption that tourists wanted everything, except the weather, to be just like home. Armed with this assumption, Santa Barbara citizens set about providing Santa Barbara with all the amenities of an Eastern city. Streetlights were electrified in 1887, a water system was developed by tunneling through the Santa Ynez Mountains and building Gibraltar Dam, parks were developed, and lovely Cabrillo Boulevard was constructed along the waterfront.

Good medical care was a high priority. Rich tourists simply would not come if they did not have medical care equal to that offered by Eastern cities. In response to this need, 50 women conducted an 1888 fund drive to raise $6,000 to build a hospital. Following an English model, this hospital was envisioned as a group of charming, cozy, home-like cottages.

Halfway through the fund drive, it became clear that a single building would be far more economical than multiple bungalows. In the face of this fiscal reality, the plan for cottages was abandoned. Nevertheless, the name Cottage Hospital was retained for the cozy, friendly impression it created.

Although access to this hospital between Bath and Carrillo on Pueblo was difficult due to unpaved roads that were impassable in wet weather, Cottage Hospital opened in December 1891. In the years to follow, Cottage Hospital has been the home of many surgical and research breakthroughs. In 1922, **Dr. William Sansum**, following up on a Canadian discovery, developed the world's first long-acting insulin to treat diabetics, spurring a decade-long migration of diabetics from all over the world to Santa Barbara.

Once hotels and amenities were established, entertainment for rich tourists was the next priority. Santa Barbara citizens expended energy developing a set of scenic journeys for tourists with time on their hands. One favorite tourist outing was a leisurely drive: past Stearns Wharf, the Dibblee Mansion (today's site of Santa Barbara City College), Castle Rock (where the harbor is today), and on to the 1856 stone lighthouse on the Mesa (today's Coast Guard housing facility) for a leisurely picnic lunch.

An important aspect of Santa Barbara's reputation as a leisurely, serene town was based on its social and cultural activities. Since its early Spanish days, Santa Barbara had been known as a town that knew how to entertain graciously. Poets, artists, and scholars were drawn to this genteel culture. One example of this is that Santa Barbara, as isolated and small as it was, became the home of California's first community theatre, the Lobero.

Jose Lobero came from Italy in 1864 and opened a saloon at State and Canon Perdido. He soon founded an orchestra that played in the saloon. From this unusual blend of leisure pursuits, recruiting citizens to stage grand opera in the saloon seemed to be a natural next step. Lobero put his considerable energy and talents into these opera productions: he designed sets and costumes, trained and directed citizens, recruited and managed the orchestra, and sang the leading roles.

Eventually, these productions outgrew the saloon. Undaunted, Lobero sought investors and got financial backing from Colonel Hollister to build a theatre using an old adobe schoolhouse for its foyer and balcony. Opening in 1872, the new theatre offered, as its first performance, an opera directed, produced, and composed by Lobero.

Although the Lobero Theatre soon became a social and cultural center of Santa Barbara, Jose Lobero lost his fortune and sank into obscurity. Fortunately for Santa Barbara, the theatre thrived. In 1924, the Community Arts Association acquired the Lobero. Since it was in serious need of renovation, they built a new Lobero Theatre. A festival was organized to celebrate its opening. This was the first Old Spanish Days Fiesta, still celebrated every August.

Jose Lobero's Brewery Saloon

Although this rush to please tourists provided many important amenities, State Street suffered. It had become dull and ugly. It would take the 1925 earthquake to force Santa Barbara to rebuild State Street with the character and charm it now exudes.

Suburbs

Some tourists never went home. Most who stayed did not want to live near the increasingly unappealing downtown. Instead, they bought large tracts outside the city in areas that were to become Montecito and Summerland.

Named "El Montecito," little mountain, by the Spanish, Montecito had been a popular rendezvous for horse thieves in the 1850s and '60s. When these gangs left the area, a number of Italian farmers came to develop small truck farms and fruit orchards. By 1888, tourists venturing outside Santa Barbara discovered a lush, lovely area of small, thriving farms, blossoming gardens, and green lawns looking a great deal like Italy.

Rich tourists were charmed. In Montecito, they had found just what they were seeking: verdant hills, great ocean views, and large tracts of cheap land close enough to Santa Barbara for services and culture, but just far enough away to maintain the serenity they desired.

Montecito's tradition as a Santa Barbara's rich, suburban neighborhood of beautiful homes and exquisite gardens was established early by these rich travelers who had found the home they were seeking.

When Charles Nordhoff described Santa Barbara, he lauded its numerous hot springs. Some of the best of these springs were located in a remote canyon in Montecito. As Montecito became the home of the rich, a luxurious resort, the Montecito Hot Springs Hotel, was built at these springs. Famous for the exotic waters, three types of mineral springs (iron, sulfur, and arsenic) were blended for guests. According to legend, this resort was so exclusive that travelers had to have at least seven digits in their bank accounts to be admitted. In 1920, fire totally destroyed the Montecito Hot Springs Hotel, but by 1923, a smaller, still luxurious, club was built that accommodated only 17 members.

In 1782, the Spanish-built Presidio had needed something to waterproof its roof. At the site of today's Summerland, the perfect material was found: a black goo seeping up through the dirt. Although this oil would eventually alter the course of Summerland's development, its early residents were spiritualists rather than oil prospectors. A real estate promoter and spiritualist, **H. L. Williams,** bought a tract of land and named the area to market its great weather and to appeal to spiritualists, among whom a book, *Summerland,* was popular.

He subdivided the land and advertised it to fellow spiritualists. Lots were 25 feet wide by 60 feet deep and were sold for $1 per frontal foot ($25). Spiritualists came and built small homes. Many of these homes had unusual architectural elements, such as staircases that led nowhere and doors opening to walls. For many years, life in Summerland centered on a séance room donated by Williams. This room survived until it was destroyed in the 1950s when the U.S. 101 freeway was built.

Initially, settlers who struck oil while digging wells cursed the gooey substance as a nuisance. By 1895, a well being drilled hit a layer of oil and gas that became the country's first full-fledged oil boom. In the pandemonium of the oil rush, the spiritualist nature of colony was lost. The lots that had recently sold for $25 were being grabbed for $7,500, 300 times their cost a few years earlier. Almost overnight, Summerland was covered by a forest of squat wooden derricks.

Seeking more oil, experts looked to the ocean. They believed that great fields of oil lay underwater in the channel between Summerland and the Channel Islands. Wharves with derricks were built out into the ocean, and Summerland became the site of the world's first sub-marine oil wells. Although production from these wharf-mounted derricks had tapered off by 1910, the forest of flimsy wooden derricks marred Summerland's beaches well into the 1920s.

As Santa Barbara citizens bid farewell to the 19th century and welcomed the new century, they looked back at incredible changes. These changes included sovereignty by three different nations and the transition from a Spanish church/military culture to a pleasing travel destination to many, and a home to some.

Forest of derricks at Summerland

Pumping oil at Summerland

Breakwater construction, seen from Castillo Point

Welcoming the 20th Century

When the railroad was completed to Ellwood in 1887, Santa Barbara celebrated. Although pleased to be finally connected to Los Angeles, Santa Barbarans still wanted easy access north to San Francisco. Citizens were distressed by the 50-mile gap in rail service between Ellwood and the mouth of the Santa Ynez River. Continually focused on securing this connection, citizens were forced to endure a long wait.

It took 14 years until Santa Barbara residents could cheer the completion of the railroad. Troubles, ranging from acquiring the necessary easements, labor problems, and engineering challenges, plagued every mile of the project. One surprising challenge was the unwillingness of certain citizens along the route to provide the necessary easements. No matter how fervently citizens wanted a railroad in Santa Barbara, everyone wanted it to be built on someone else's land. Property owners did not welcome the railroad on or near their land, and complained about the railroad's noise and dirt. Before all required easements had been secured, some citizens had even sued to stop the railroad from being built.

Once this challenge had been overcome, labor problems began. Plenty of men signed up to work. Unfortunately, keeping them was another matter entirely. The temptations offered by the raucous community of saloonkeepers, prostitutes, con men, and gamblers that followed the progress of the railroad were too appealing to many of these workers. As a result of these enticing diversions, many workers were in no shape to work when morning came. Although the railroad managers could not stop these entrepreneurs from following the workers, they did eventually retaliate by paying workers in script that was redeemable only at the company store.

In addition to the problems posed by landowners and an unstable workforce, this project faced huge engineering challenges. A 660-foot trestle had to be built across Dos Pueblos Canyon.

Additionally, this undertaking required the construction of a large railroad culvert near El Capitan and two 800-foot tunnels that had to be blasted through mountains near Point Arguello.

Despite these difficulties, Santa Barbara's isolation from northern destinations ended on March 31, 1901 amid citywide elation. As citizens waited with flowers and bands to celebrate the arrival of the first train, Frank Sands, the editor of the *Daily News*, captured the enthusiastic optimism of the day by crowing, "Santa Barbara is no longer on a side track. Nothing can stop us now!"

Four trains arrived each day and instantly overshadowed all other forms of transportation to Santa Barbara. This first day of railroad service marked the last trip of the stagecoach that had labored over San Marcos Pass to bridge the gap in rail service. It also had a significant negative impact on the number of travelers arriving by ship. Even though the train trip from Los Angeles often took 10 hours, most travelers far preferred it to ocean travel. They were willing to pay the hefty one-way rates of 50 cents to Goleta, $3.70 to Lompoc and $11.85 first-class/$9 coach to San Francisco.

With the completion of the railroad, visitors no longer had to endure long boat or stagecoach rides to reach Santa Barbara. As a stop along the railroad route, Santa Barbara could now participate in a never-ending flow of travelers exploring California. It marked an end to leisurely days and old traditions as Santa Barbara citizens jumped joyfully into mainstream California. They bid a cheerful farewell to their isolation and set to work transforming their town into a resort of world renown.

The Potter Hotel

To become a world-class resort, Santa Barbara needed world-class hotels. Santa Barbara hotels simply could not offer enough luxury accommodations. The Arlington Hotel on State Street had established Santa Barbara as a winter resort for the wealthy when it was built a quarter of a century before, but it was neither large nor elegant enough for the new influx of travelers brought by the railroad.

A committee of Santa Barbara citizens knew that they must attract development for the hotel their town needed. They set out to entice **Milo Potter**, owner of the Van Nuys Hotel, with an offer he could not refuse. The committee offered to sell him a choice 36-acre lot with 2-block frontage on Cabrillo Street between Chapala and Bath Streets. The deal was concluded quickly. By 1902, Santa Barbara had a new $150,000, 600-room palace, the Potter Hotel. With one of California's most fashionable hotels, Santa Barbara was ready to greet its guests.

And what a hotel it was! Rooms were exquisite and the gardens luxurious. Grounds boasted 30,000 rose bushes, acres of lilies and violets, and a famous mile of red geraniums. Guests were invited to pick their own asparagus and artichokes. The Avenue of Palms, leading from the hotel's front towers to the beach 500 feet away, set the stage for exotic elegance. (Though the Potter is long gone, these palms still thrive.)

Potter did not settle for just a grand hotel and lush grounds. He also built a separate hotel for employees, a Potter Garage for cars, and tracks for private railroad cars to deposit their rich owners at the elegant entrance and then park nearby. To ensure his restaurant served only the finest food, he also established Potter Ranch in Goleta. Here, he planted extensive vegetable gardens and stocked it with 60,000 pigeons and chickens. Hotel advertising boasted that: "The Potter Ranch keeps 400 little Roasting Pigs at all times, and dairy products are supplied by 175 blooded cows. We have the finest homegrown vegetables all year round."

Aware that guests wanted more than good food and ocean views, he also built the Potter Country Club, complete with a racetrack, polo grounds, and a 9-hole golf course.

Unfortunately, the establishment of the Potter Hotel marked the demise of one of Santa Barbara's most famous sulfur springs at Burton Mound, adjacent to the hotel. The springs had played an important role in the region for centuries. The Chumash who settled at Burton Mound enjoyed the curative powers of its springs. When the Spanish arrived, sailors fighting scurvy found a cure in these springs and by the mid-1880s it had become a popular bathing spot. Initially, Potter tried to capitalize on the sulfur springs by

The Potter Hotel

having its water pumped into the hotel's main lobby. Unfortunately, guests complained about the strong sulfuric smell. He not only stopped pumping the water into the lobby, but he also sealed off the springs by filling the entire area with tons of cement.

When citizens expressed dismay, he rationalized the loss by saying that he was doing Santa Barbara a favor: the hot springs were for the ill, and Santa Barbara should serve the rich and healthy. "Santa Barbara should not be a Mecca for hypochondriacs anyway," Potter said. "We have the finest year-round climate in the world here, so let's give the healthy a chance to enjoy it."

Despite the hefty rates of $3 per day in the summer and $4 and up during the winter (not including food), the Potter Hotel was an instant success. The rich came and spent their money there and throughout the town. Some who came and spent were the Carnegies, Rockefellers, Astors, and McCormicks. Not unexpectedly, many also stayed and built estates in Montecito.

In addition to setting a new standard of elegance, the Potter Hotel firmly established Santa Barbara as a place to play rather than recuperate. Milo Potter came to Santa Barbara with the intention of creating a hotel that would cater to healthy, fun-loving, rich tourists, and he did just that.

Hotel Fires

In just over a decade, both the Arlington and the Potter Hotels burned. A blaze of unknown origin destroyed the Arlington on the evening of August 15, 1909. While guests were retrieving their belongings, the elevator operator, Robert Klein, kept the elevator running until he collapsed of a heart attack. In another heroic tale, a multimillionaire from Los Angeles drove his limousine all night transporting guests to private homes where they were welcomed.

As soon as it became clear that the hotel was doomed, volunteer firefighters with primitive equipment concentrated on saving the Annex at Chapala and Victoria. Despite the bombardment of wind-borne embers and the searing heat of the fire, the Annex, a multi-gabled, four-story, wooden firetrap was saved.

Before the fire cooled, guests began to worry about their possessions. Fortunes had been placed into the hotel safe. The safe was dragged to today's location of the Arlington Box Office. For five days it cooled and the town wondered if anything had survived. Crowds watched as it was opened. A great sign of relief went up as it was discovered that nothing, neither jewels nor paper currency, had been damaged.

Although the original Arlington had been destroyed, 40 percent of the $100,000 loss was covered by insurance. The "New" Arlington was built two years later. While the Arlington had established Santa Barbara as a tourist destination, the New Arlington catered to a more sedate clientele, replete with tea dances and a restaurant for men only. This New Arlington never prospered. It seems that the sporting set preferred the less conservative Potter Hotel.

The New Arlington was open just over a decade. It was damaged in the June 29, 1925 earthquake when the 60,000-gallon water tank

69

Potter Hotel destroyed by Fire in 1921

killed two when it toppled from a tower and through the ceiling of some deluxe suites. As it was not prospering, the New Arlington was razed and the Annex was destroyed a few years later.

The glory of the Potter Hotel was short-lived—it was open only 19 years, from 1902 until 1921. On April 13, 1921, a 50-mph gale hit the coast and fanned a fire that destroyed the hotel. Razor-sharp sheet metal roof tiles were whipped off and flung for blocks. When it was over, only the palms remained standing.

The Potter Hotel was never rebuilt. Although it was destroyed by the fire, its decline had already begun. World War I played a part in this decline, but a more significant contributor was the advent of the automobile. Less than two decades after Santa Barbara citizens had cheered its arrival, the importance of the railroad had diminished, and the automobile had become the transportation of choice. The tourists who came by auto brought about a shift in Santa Barbara's need for hotel accommodations. The opulent Potter Hotel, located next to the railroad, no longer addressed these needs.

The fire that destroyed the Potter brought the end of an era. Despite its short life, it had a significant role in Santa Barbara's story. It solidified the town's reputation as the gracious destination for well-heeled tourists and enticed affluent travelers from all over the world.

Shopping at Its Best

The influx of affluent visitors resulted in sophisticated amenities that were enjoyed by tourists and citizens, alike. An example of this was the group of elegant retail businesses that thrived on State Street between Haley and Ortega at the turn of the century. It began when **Jacob Eisenberg**, a German immigrant, came to Santa Barbara in 1898 and never left. Eisenberg's offered affluent shoppers elegant millinery and stylish, custom-made clothing for both men and women. He became the respected leader of many Santa Barbara retailers who credited Eisenberg with all they knew about the art of salesmanship. He shared his profits with his long-time employees and was proudest of his success in persuading businesses to close early on Saturdays to give their clerks some time with their families.

Another famous shop, Diehl's Grocery at 827 State Street, catered to the growing Santa Barbara carriage trade. Diehl's was founded in 1891 by three German brothers and reigned for over 40 years as one of the premier gourmet food businesses in the world. It was established to cater to Montecito's rich. When they arrived for the winter, their butlers and housekeepers came immediately to Diehl's to provision. As wealthy patrons themselves began to browse the gourmet items from exotic countries, its soda fountain became the elegant place to meet for lunch or tea.

Diehl's symbolized a golden era of money, leisure, and servants and capitalized on a passion for exotic foods served elegantly on sterling, crystal, linen, and bone china. Eventually, Diehl's gained worldwide fame through its exotic catalog, *A Dictionary of Good Things to Eat*, which allowed affluent customers to order Diehl's food from anywhere in the world.

Diehl's was a genteel establishment that freely offered credit to its wealthy patrons. The 1929 Crash left Diehl's with enormous unpaid bills and significantly reduced numbers of patrons who could still afford to shop there. The seeds of its decline were sown. When it finally closed in 1940, Diehl's world of butlers and housekeepers. had ended forever.

Diehl's Grocery at 827 State Street

Almost Hollywood

Briefly, Santa Barbara housed the world's largest movie studio. In 1910 the first movie company arrived, and by 1911, there were 13 movie companies located in Santa Barbara. During this brief time, Santa Barbara's mountains and beaches portrayed locations as diverse as South Sea islands and the Alps. The largest movie company, American Film Manufacturing (known as Flying A), at State and Mission Streets, built what is believed to be the world's first indoor movie set, and may have originated the first animated cartoons. When it was completed in 1913, it was the largest movie lot in the world.

By 1918, just eight years after the first moviemakers had arrived, they were moving south. They needed more sun and a city with big buildings to serve as backgrounds for their films depicting urban settings. Santa Barbara was unable to meet these needs, and bid goodbye to its brief time in the spotlight.

Flying A's lot at Chapala and Mission Streets

The Great Harbor Debate

To become a port and playground for the growing numbers of boaters in Southern California, Santa Barbara needed a safe harbor. For decades, Santa Barbara citizens had wanted this harbor. **Major Max Fleischmann**, the yeast magnate and an avid boater, wanted to help Santa Barbara realize this dream. He offered the city $200,000 to build the harbor, with the condition that the city match this donation. Santa Barbara voters enthusiastically supported a bond to raise the remaining $200,000.

That was the easy part. The location of this harbor was far more controversial. Max and other wealthy landowners wanted the harbor built at Castle Rock (its current location). Others, including engineers and Yacht Club members, protested. They knew the prevailing currents would continually silt up the harbor. They predicted enormous dredging costs each year to keep the harbor open, and recommended Salt Pond, the location of today's Bird Refuge, instead. In addition to providing a location that would be far easier to maintain, Salt Pond would have been less costly to build since the city already owned it. In 1909, the city had purchased Salt Pond and 31 contiguous acres for $7,364.

Despite solid arguments in favor of the Salt Pond location, Max Fleischmann's money spoke loudest his recommended location was selected. The engineers and Yacht Club members were later proven right. A large dredge still works, at a cost of approximately $2 million per year, to rid the harbor of sand brought by the littoral drift.

Harbor, protected by Breakwater, 1930s

Santa Barbara's Flourishing Chinatown

Until 1925, Santa Barbara had a flourishing Chinatown on Canon Perdido between State and Santa Barbara Streets. Most residents had come to California to labor on the railroad or in the gold fields, and worked in Santa Barbara as houseboys, laundrymen, or laborers in the vineyards. Although most were solid, hard-working citizens, it was their "tongs," or secret societies, that made the headlines during the early decades of the 20th century. Conflicts between these tongs provided citizens all the elements of a Hollywood crime movie: hit men, gambling, opium, and murder.

In Santa Barbara, two powerful tongs, Hop Sing and Bing Kong, ran lucrative gambling and opium businesses with an iron hand. The center of these businesses was the joss house and Chinese Masonic Temple at 27 East Canon Perdido, near the Lobero Theatre. The gambling hall upstairs was extremely lucrative. Legend has it that the profit was 90 cents of each dollar collected. This illegal operation was raided periodically when police coffers needed to be replenished.

The two tongs had negotiated a shared lease on the joss house and Masonic Temple: each tong had the lease for a year and passed it to their rival for the next year. This system worked well until 1925, when the Hop Sing Tong refused to give up the lease when their year was up.

The Bing Kong tong responded by hiring two assassins from San Francisco to kill the leader of the Hop Sing. The assassins were successful and he was gunned down in front of the Lobero Theatre just as patrons were leaving a performance. With many shocked theatergoers as witnesses, the assassins were arrested immediately. They were released when their crafty lawyer proved witnesses could not identify them in a roomful of other Chinese men.

By the late 1920s, a portion of Chinatown, including the infamous joss house and Masonic Temple, was demolished to make room for today's Post Office. The Chinese community members dispersed, and Santa Barbara's Chinatown ceased to exist.

Tragedies at Honda

The early 20th century also saw three terrible accidents at Honda, on the rocky coast between Point Arguello and the mouth of the Santa Ynez River. The first was the tragic derailment of a train on May 11, 1907. Most passengers were Shriners and their families on a sight-seeing trip to San Francisco. The locomotive's wheels jumped the rails and cars were flung all around. When they settled, many cars were piled on top of each other. Thirty-six people died, and hundreds were seriously injured. The carnage horrified Santa Barbara citizens.

Only four years later, in 1911, the *Santa Rosa* sank at Honda, and in 1923 Honda was the scene of the worst multiple shipwreck in marine history when 7 U. S. Navy destroyers sank. The commander of the squadron did not trust his new-fangled RDF (Radio Direction Finder) in the fog and used his dead reckoning calculations to identify the eastward turn in the coast at Pt. Arguello. He ordered all ships to travel in close formation and, turning too soon, went aground on the rocky shoals. Six others followed and sank. Only those ships whose captains disobeyed the close-formation order survived.

Destroyers aground at Honda

The early 1900s brought great changes to Santa Barbara. It brought the railroad, wealthy tourists, the opulent Potter, and the exquisite shops demanded by the affluent. It also brought the movie industry, immigrants, the automobile with a new type of tourist, devastating fires, and tragedies at Honda. After such momentous events, many expected a lull. Instead, in 1925, a devastating earthquake hit Santa Barbara and ushered in an era of even more rapid change.

Earthquake Spurs Transformation

While many citizens were enjoying Santa Barbara's reputation as a favorite destination of rich travelers, some were beginning to notice that their beloved town had lost its charm. Instead, it looked like many Eastern towns. Convinced that the charm and uniqueness of Santa Barbara could be recaptured only by reviving its Spanish roots, these locals, led by **Bernard Hoffmann** and **Pearl Chase**, began trying to convince property owners to add white stucco walls and red tile roofs to their buildings.

While this plea initially fell on deaf ears, Santa Barbara citizens were forced to rebuild when, on June 29, 1925, a devastating earthquake destroyed much of the town. While the initial quake was centered in a fault just offshore, two aftershocks five minutes apart, centered in the nearby foothills, did most of the damage. Soon after the quake, a fire broke out that nearly destroyed what was left of

New Arlington Hotel destroyed by Earthquake

Devastation on State Street

Santa Barbara. Marines who had arrived to deal with the earthquake damage are credited with containing this fire and saving large portions of the town.

Most downtown buildings were destroyed or badly damaged. Even buildings that did not appear to be damaged needed a great deal of work before they could be used again. Luckily, the quake hit at 6:23 a.m. while many slept, and only 12 people were killed.

This quake gave Santa Barbara the initial push it needed to begin a welcome transformation. As nearly all of the frame Victorian buildings were destroyed, some saw this as a golden opportunity to rebuild Santa Barbara into a Spanish-like town, using stronger adobe-like materials, arches, and tile roofs.

Not everyone agreed and, initially, many rebuilt buildings looked much as they had before the quake. Nevertheless, powerful visionaries led by Hoffmann and Chase relentlessly sought to rebuild to a Spanish-style conformity. Although it took decades to implement the new architectural direction, the damage wreaked by the earthquake spurred the initial impetus toward the transformation of Santa Barbara and the development of State Street into one of the most beautiful and distinctive business streets in the United States.

Padres at Mission inspecting Earthquake damage

Santa Barbara Visionaries

Bernard Hoffmann was a successful East Coast engineer who came to Santa Barbara in 1919 with his 12-year old daughter, Margaret, who was suffering from incurable juvenile diabetes. He was following the foremost specialist in this field, **Dr. Nathaniel Bowditch Potter**, who had just moved his clinic from New York City to Santa Barbara. Although Potter died that year, **Dr. W. D. Sansum** continued Potter's research in a wing of Cottage Hospital. As soon as insulin was discovered, Sansum began manufacturing and testing it on his 20 patients. Margaret was one of the lucky 20, and she recovered completely.

Hoffmann began making a profound impact on the look of Santa Barbara even before the earthquake. He purchased Santa Barbara's most valued remnant of Spanish days, the Casa De la Guerra, the social center of Spanish Santa Barbara built in the 1820s by Jose De la Guerra, Comandante of the Presidio.

Although the granddaughters of De la Guerra were still living in the adobe, it was rapidly decaying. Rather than knocking it down, Hoffmann used it and the surrounding area to develop a charming cluster of shops, courtyards, walkways, and arches. By 1924, El Paseo, the first pedestrian mall west of the Mississippi, was completed. This vanguard of Santa Barbara's new look set a standard for much of the post-earthquake rebuilding, and still plays a central role in downtown Santa Barbara.

After the earthquake, Hoffmann led the rebuilding of Santa Barbara. He chaired many committees, including the powerful Architectural Advisory Committee, charged with approving all commercial reconstruction plans. He used this power to support the use of Spanish Revival architecture. Opposition to this was reduced for two reasons:

First, while most downtown buildings had tumbled during the earthquake, Hoffmann's El Paseo had survived unscathed. Seeking earthquake-proof buildings, many property owners agreed that buildings using adobe-like materials were stronger. Additionally,

Hoffmann offered property owners the free services of a team of Spanish Revival architects.

Slowly, Spanish-style buildings began to dot the devastated downtown.

Although Hoffmann left Santa Barbara in 1927, the seeds of a new Santa Barbara had been planted. The project was left to powerful, determined, irascible, and extremely effective **Pearl Chase** to get the job done. Many believe Chase created the beautiful town Santa Barbara is today.

Pearl Chase

After Hoffmann left, Chase took over his mission as a zealous, tireless, one-person committee and the chairperson of innumerable community organizations. Her passions included the beautification of Santa Barbara, the protection of Chumash interests, environmental concerns, preservation of Santa Barbara's historical buildings, and the adoption of Spanish-style architecture.

One example of her ability to wage battle successfully against powerful foes is her victory over the Standard Oil Company. Standard Oil planned to build a gas station on the plot where Santa Barbara's historic Moreton Bay fig was growing. Chase won, and the world-famous tree still thrives and delights residents and visitors, alike.

She accomplished goals by her sheer force of will, her reputation for getting her way at all costs, and her powerful connections. Many did not like being forced to do as Chase dictated, but few can deny her positive impact on the Santa Barbara we know today.

One of the best results of the 1925 earthquake, Santa Barbara's County Courthouse, was completed in 1929. It was rebuilt with hand-chiseled sandstone from Refugio on its original site. Built in a Spanish-Moorish style at a cost of $1.5 million, this courthouse is considered by many to be the loveliest in the United States.

Santa Barbara's University

Despite Santa Barbara's slow start in establishing schools, higher education took an important leap forward during the early years of the 20th century. Higher education in Santa Barbara had begun when **Anna Sophia Cabot Blake** arrived in Santa Barbara in 1890 to begin Blake's Normal School. It was so successful that, in 1909, the State Board of Education funded a campus on the Riviera, portions of which house today's Riviera Theatre. The establishment of this school spurred the development of the adjacent area and, by 1913, the Riviera neighborhood had been established. One landowner adjacent to the school built a two-story house and two bungalows intended to house 40 faculty and students. When neither students nor faculty rented these facilities, he converted his buildings to a hotel, the El Encanto, still one of Santa Barbara's finest.

Before long the school, renamed Santa Barbara State Teachers College (SBSTC), had grown so rapidly that more space was needed. Surrounded by homes, expansion at the Riviera site was impossible, and a new larger campus was sought.

When the earthquake destroyed an imposing stone mansion, the Dibblee's Punta Del Castillo, on the cliff overlooking the harbor, the land was available. By 1932, the state had purchased this land for a new campus of the SBSTC. At this time, the Great Depression was at its peak. Crews employed under the Works Progress Administration (WPA), funded through Franklin Roosevelt's New Deal, cleared the remains of the mansion, using the stone to build the retaining wall on Cliff Drive. The first building of the new campus was completed in 1941.

Construction stopped during World War II. At war's end the college, later to become the University of California, Santa Barbara, moved to its present location near Goleta, at the vacated Marine Corps training station.

The Great Depression

The rebuilding and beautification of Santa Barbara was aided by New Deal funding designed to combat the unemployment of the Great Depression. **Thomas Storke**, editor and publisher of the *Santa Barbara News-Press*, contended that his swing vote for Roosevelt's nomination at the 1932 Democratic National Convention resulted in $22 million in New Deal funding for Santa Barbara. He may have been correct, for Santa Barbara certainly did receive a huge amount of relief funding for a town of only 35,000 residents. With this money, Santa Barbara got the County Bowl, the National Guard Armory, the Administration Building of Santa Barbara City College, the filtration plant at Sheffield Reservoir, Gibraltar Road, and Laguna Park.

Despite all this funding, many were still unemployed. In addition to Santa Barbara locals, a large number of single homeless men had gravitated west to Santa Barbara, seeking opportunity and milder weather. Eventually, a unique village was established when they began camping on the estate of **Lillian Child**, at the present location of the Santa Barbara Zoo. She welcomed them, and soon there were 30 shacks and a self-governing community with an elected mayor. When Child died in 1951, the land was deeded to the Santa Barbara Foundation under the condition that the residents could stay. It was 1963 before they had relocated and the Zoo was built.

The first few decades of the 20th century also brought racial tensions to Santa Barbara. A symbol of this tension was the Ku Klux Klan, a group that professed hatred of all who were foreign or Catholic. The Klan burned crosses, and 100-car caravans cruised State Street threatening Mexicans. In 1923, a group of Klansmen threatened to assault a Mexican-American man on Mexican Independence Day. A man who was a descendent of one of the Presidio soldiers intervened and brandished his gun at the Klansmen. Although he was arrested for carrying a gun, the district attorney refused to prosecute him; instead, he blasted the Klan in Santa Barbara. Additionally, the city prohibited police officers from joining the Klan.

These early years of the 20th century brought Santa Barbara destruction from its devastating earthquake, rebirth as a Spanish town, and establishment of important city institutions. A powerful undercurrent of intolerance also marked these years. Together, these forces established the roots of today's Santa Barbara.

A Santa Barbara Dilemma:
To Grow or Not to Grow?

No longer isolated, Santa Barbara played a unique role in World War II. On February 23, 1942, a Japanese submarine attacked the oil facilities at Ellwood, on the western outskirts of Goleta. For 40 minutes, the Japanese fired 25 shells toward the shore. Much of the ordnance did not explode on impact, and the resulting damage was less than $500. The submarine left Santa Barbara before there was time for any response from the Coast Guard. Rumor had it that the commander of the Japanese submarine had been fired from the Ellwood facility and had come back to Santa Barbara for revenge. This barrage constituted the only Japanese attack on the California coast.

In early March 1942, the United States government ordered that all individuals of Japanese descent, including those who were U.S. citizens, turn themselves in to be relocated. On April 30, approximately 700 men, women, and children brought all the belongings that they could carry to the American Legion Hall on Cabrillo Boulevard. From there they were taken to primitive and overcrowded camps to wait out the war.

Santa Barbara citizens found themselves at the center of a great deal of military activity for the duration of the war. Marines set up quarters in Goleta at today's site of the University of California so that they could train at the new airport. They significantly enlarged the runways and filled in much of the Goleta Slough. Unfortunately, they filled it in by leveling Mescaltitlan Island, the mound in the middle of the slough that had been the site of one of the area's largest Chumash settlements. The Army established Camp Cook near Lompoc, the future site of today's Vandenberg Air Force Base and also took over the Biltmore and Miramar hotels for recreational needs. The Navy took control of the waterfront and moved into the Naval Reserve Building.

Ships at Navy Pier (now City Pier) in WW II

They asked local fishermen to catch as many sharks as possible, for shark liver was thought to improve night vision and the blood of injured servicemen. Santa Barbara's premiere commercial fishing family, the Castagnolas, supplied much of this shark catch.

The military also opened Hoff General Hospital in Santa Barbara, where wounded servicemen were examined before returning to action. Approximately 28,000 servicemen had their first visit to Santa Barbara via Hoff Hospital.

And the People Came

Some who saw Santa Barbara during World War II remembered and returned after the war. Many bought homes in Santa Barbara's first low-cost housing development: truck farms and oil derricks on the Mesa had been bulldozed to make room for a large number of modest homes.

Between 1940 and 1950, Santa Barbara's population grew by 10,000. Despite the low-cost housing on the Mesa, housing was scarce, and rents skyrocketed. The City Council enacted an emergency rent control ordinance in hopes of keeping costs down.

This era of rapid growth ushered in a host of problems. Traffic increased so much that traffic lights had to be installed on State Street, and by 1946 U.S. Highway 101 was running through Santa Barbara.

More serious than traffic or housing was Santa Barbara's water problem. When the Gibraltar Dam was completed in 1920, most believed that all of Santa Barbara's water problems had been solved. By 1946, in the midst of both the post-war population growth and a drought, it was clear that Santa Barbara had a huge water problem. The Fiesta was cancelled that year, and Montecito officials threatened to jail residents who used more than their allotment of water.

A solution, enthusiastically supported by *Santa Barbara News-Press* publisher Thomas Storke, was formulated and approved: Cachuma Reservoir would be built, at a total cost of $43 million, much of it from Federal loans. When construction was complete in 1956, leaders envisioned limitless growth for the South Coast.

Although much of Santa Barbara's growth in the years after World War II did come from those who had passed through during the war, other groups were actively recruited during these years. The event that had the most significant single impact on Santa Barbara's population was the decision to convert the 408 acres near the airport that the Marines had used during the war into the University of California, Santa Barbara (UCSB) campus. Thomas Storke, a regent for the University of California, focused his considerable power on getting the federal land transferred, aiding the creation of UCSB.

From the beginning, the university had a major impact on the region. Enrollments were larger than anticipated, and students flooded into the area. Large numbers of staff also were hired, and Goleta cleared some of California's richest agricultural land to build homes for them. Almost immediately, UCSB emerged as the county's largest employer.

In addition to the growth and employment it generated, UCSB had a significant impact on the development of Santa Barbara by providing cultural opportunities, intellectual energy, and huge numbers of young people. Despite the difficult Viet Nam years marked by anti-war demonstrations and the burning of Isla Vista's Bank of America, most agree that Thomas Storke's visionary advocacy of the establishment of a major university had a significantly positive impact on Santa Barbara.

Business Wooed, while Oil Companies Rejected

At the same time UCSB was being established, city promoters were actively recruiting corporations. They intended to change Santa Barbara's reputation as a resort town unfriendly to business. The word was sent East: clean businesses that would not ruin Santa Barbara's charm were welcome. By 1961, Aerophysics, Raytheon, and General Motor's Delco Research Division had relocated to the Santa Barbara area.

To preserve Santa Barbara's beauty so that tourists would continue to come and spend, citizens took an aggressive anti-oil stand. When, in 1954, the State of California proposed opening the coast from the high water mark to three miles offshore to petroleum developers, Santa Barbara sought and was granted a special exemption. The City also banned all oil drilling within the city limits.

It looked as if Santa Barbara was winning its battle against the oil companies until technological advances in the 1960s made it profitable to drill oil from platforms more than three miles offshore, the waters under federal jurisdiction. A consortium led by Union Oil Company paid $61.4 million in 1968 for an offshore tract 5.5 miles off the coast of Carpinteria. Despite well-known fragile subsurface geological conditions, Union Oil was given special permission to bypass fundamental safety precautions.

The fragile ocean bottom was ruptured, and by January 28, 1969, the sea around the platform was boiling with oil. In 100 days, 77,000 barrels of oil burst from the rupture, coating the coastline with crude oil from Hope Ranch to Carpinteria out to the Channel Islands. Wildlife died by the tens of thousands, while television coverage broadcast Santa Barbara's woes all over the world.

This oil spill spawned a rapid-fire series of reactions. President Richard Nixon signed the National Environmental Protection Act, and California created the California Coastal Commission and the California Environmental Quality Act. These laws radically changed the rules for development in California. Additionally, environmental groups such as GOO! (Get Oil Out!), the Community Environmental Council, the Environmental Defense Center, and UCSB's Environmental Studies Program were established.

Locally, City Council reacted by refusing to renew its Stearns Wharf lease with the local fishermen, **George** and **Mario Castagnola**, because they had rented much of the wharf to oil support industries. In 1973, shortly after the lease was cancelled, the Castagnolas' Harbor restaurant and much of the wharf burned. The damaged part of the wharf remained unsafe and unused for a decade before it was rebuilt. (When the wharf burned again in 1998, it was rebuilt almost immediately.)

This environmental passion also sowed the seeds of a battle that still rages between commercial fishermen and environmental advocates. Santa Barbara's harbor is unusual in Southern California for its large fleet of commercial fishing vessels. The presence of a working fishing fleet adds character and charm to Santa Barbara's waterfront that is not present in most other California marinas. Nevertheless, due to serious environmental concerns about fish and wildlife in the Santa Barbara Channel, the future viability of this fleet is in question.

Santa Barbara Citizens vs. the Developers

Since its earliest years, Santa Barbara's citizens railed against its isolation and sought growth. They lamented lagging behind other rapidly growing Southern California towns. Finally, by the late 1940s, many believed that Santa Barbara's isolation was finally over and growth and prosperity were on the horizon: new homes on the

Mesa were sold immediately, UCSB was thriving, and businesses had begun selecting Santa Barbara as their home. Proposals to transform Santa Barbara into a large, thriving metropolis included:

- The Southern Pacific and the Hyatt Corporation proposal for a 1,000-room waterfront hotel and resort that would necessitate re-routing Cabrillo Boulevard.

- An eight-story, twin-tower high-rise where Alice Keck Memorial Gardens is today.

- The expansion of Stearns Wharf into a 90,000 square foot, 70-store shopping center.

- Plans for converting two blocks of downtown State Street into an enclosed shopping mall.

And the list went on.

Suddenly, opinion in Santa Barbara shifted. Some believe it was the terrible oil spill that illustrated the damage developers could do to Santa Barbara. Others believe that it was the dawning recognition by many that the character of the town would be lost if large commercial developments were approved. Throughout the city, a resolve to fight to retain Santa Barbara's small town charm germinated and grew.

For whatever combination of reasons, Santa Barbara citizens began to say, "No!" Wealthy citizens purchased land to protect it from developers; young environmentalists enrolled government agencies to fight the developers; and voters elected candidates who would support their anti-development stance.

By the 1970s, developers' plans were routinely being denied. In Goleta, developments that had been approved by the County Board of Supervisors were denied water meters. In Santa Barbara, an important study, *The Effects of Urban Growth*, analyzed the amount of growth the town's air, land, traffic, housing, and tax base could sustain. Results indicated that, although zoning would allow population to increase to 170,000, Santa Barbara's resources could sustain only 85,000. This report recommended a limitation on new jobs in the city. Ignoring this report, in 1975, the City Council instead decided to limit the number of new houses permitted.

In the ensuing years, as the number of jobs in Santa Barbara grew and the number of homes remained stable, Santa Barbara experienced shocking inflation in the prices of homes. Although City Council passed an ordinance in 1988 that limited commercial growth, the search for affordable housing in Santa Barbara continues to plague the city. Until a solution is found, the highways out of Santa Barbara, both north to Lompoc and south to Ventura and Oxnard, continue to be clogged day and evening as Santa Barbara workers commute to affordable homes outside Santa Barbara.

World-Class Resort

While residents fought developers, Santa Barbara's reputation as a great travel destination continued to grow. By the closing years of the 20th century, Santa Barbara had emerged as a world-class resort. Identified as the major economic force, tourism generates over a billion dollars in revenue, over 20,000 jobs, almost $80 million in tax revenues, and over $350 million in profits to local businesses each year. Its unique and luxurious hotels and inns, including the Biltmore, San Ysidro Ranch, El Encanto, Bacara, Fess Parker's Doubletree, and the Simpson House, North America's only AAA Five Diamond Inn, lure visitors from all over the world.

Once here, they play! Opportunities for ocean sports, camping, bicycling, and hiking adventures abound, while unparalleled art, music, and theatre events continuously thrill visitors. And, after a busy day enjoying the culture and natural wonders of Santa Barbara, some of the best restaurants in California revive and delight visitors.

Whether a resident or visitor, it is no surprise that Santa Barbara is known worldwide as a great place to enjoy. Although much of the credit for this goes to its stunning coastline, paralleled by gentle mountains, acknowledgement must go to those who lived and loved here. These individuals shaped the raw pastoral Spanish village into a town that remains a rare combination of sophistication and small town charm.

Santa Barbara County Courthouse

Index

Daniel Hill 24
Bernard Hoffmann 77, 80-82
Charles Hollister 49, 57, 58, 60
Honda 75,76
Hop Sing 75

L

Jose Lobero 60

M

Mexican-American War 27-32
Mission 8, 10-13, 21-24
William Mitchell 29, 30
Montecito 61, 62
Moreton Bay fig 55, 82
Joaquin Murrieta 44

N

Neophytes 10, 12, 22, 23
Charles Nordhoff 56, 57, 62

O

Oil 63, 88, 89
SS *Orizaba* 53, 58
Ortega 7, 8, 13, 14, 38
Outlaws 41-44, 61

P

Packard 38, 39
Padre Fermin de Lasuen 10
Pio Pico 24, 31, 32
Salomon Pico 42

Pirates 16-18, 44
Milo Potter 67, 69
Potter Hotel 66-70
Jack Powers 42
Presidio 7-10, 13

R

Railroad 40, 50-52, 65, 66
Ranchos 12, 21, 24, 25, 40, 46
Riviera 82
Alfred Robinson 26

S

Saint Barbara 6, 8, 10
Dr. William Sansum 59, 80
Secularization 23-25
Padre Junipero Serra 7, 8, 10
John Smith 38
Smuggling 14, 19, 25, 26
Joaquin Solis 28
Steamers 39, 40, 52-54
John P. Stearns 49, 54
Stearns Wharf 54, 89
Robert Stockton 29, 30
Thomas Storke 83, 87
Survey 36

T

Theodore Talbot 30, 32
Trapping 18, 19
Tulare 8, 21, 22

Sources

Writing about one's home is especially difficult. Everyday, walking the streets of this fascinating town, there is the constant awareness of all the wonderful stories and people that have not been included. I can only hope that you use this HarborTown History as the starting point for your exploration of the tales and landmarks of this grand city.

You may want to begin your journey by visiting the knowledgeable and committed folks at The Santa Barbara Historical Museum at Garden and De la Guerra Streets and reading the following books:

Santa Barbara-Tierra Adora: A Community History by Lawrence Hill and Marion Parks, 1930. Published by: Security-First National Bank.

Historical Highlights of Santa Barbara by Walker A. Tomkins and Russell A. Ruiz. Published by: Santa Barbara National Bank, 1970.

Santa Barbara Neighborhoods by Walker A. Tomkins. Published by: Santa Barbara Board of Realtors, 1989. Printed by Schauer Printing Studios, Santa Barabara.

Santa Barbara County—California's Wonderful Corner by Walker A. Tompkins. Sanddollar Press, Santa Barbara, 1962, second printing, 1975. (Previously published in 1962 by McNally and Loftin under title, **California's Wonderful Corner**.)

Santa Barbara's Yesterdays by Walker A. Tompkins. A Cal-Text Book. McNally and Loftin, Santa Barbara, 1962.

Santa Barbara History Makers by Walker A. Tompkins. McNally and Loftin, Santa Barbara, 1983.

Early Days of Santa Barbara by Walter S. Hawley. Santa Barbara Heritage, Third Edition, 1987.

California Edition by Thomas Storke in collaboration with Walker A. Tompkins. Western Lore Press, Second Edition, 1958.